"This book is grounded in the latest brain science, as we ... being wonderfully friendly, encouraging, and practical. It shows readers how to stay out of dead-end conflicts and instead light up the neural circuits of empathy, skillful communication, and love. A marvelous resource."

—Rick Hanson, PhD, author of *Buddha's Brain*

"I really enjoyed this book and learned a lot from it that I can use as a therapist. Stan Tatkin is a great innovator. This book is a must for every couples' therapist's library."

—John Gottman, author of *The Science of Trust*

"If you feel lost, confused or alone in your relationship, get this book right now. You will finally make sense out of chaos and pain. This is your map to go from frustration and insecurity to realize the potential of why you initially got together. Stan Tatkin's insightful book will teach you to work as a team to make your relationship journey safe, engaging, and deeply satisfying."

—Peter Pearson, PhD, couples therapy specialist and cofounder of The Couples Institute in Menlo Park, CA

"Stan Tatkin shows how our couple relationships would look if we took seriously what attachment theory and neuroscience research has taught us."

—Dan Wile, author of *After the Honeymoon*

"*Wired for Love* challenges partners to experience their relationship in a totally new way. Partners will learn how to engage positively as a couple to help each other feel safe and secure by following the relationship exercises suggested in this exciting new book. In clear, concise language, Tatkin describes the ways that partners can understand and become experts on one another. He suggests building a "couple bubble" wherein each partner is the most important person in the other's life, the one individual on whom the partner can always count."

> —Marion F. Solomon, director of clinical training at Lifespan Learning Institute and author of *Narcissism and Intimacy, Lean on Me*, and other books

"Read this book to discover a multitude of new ways to enliven your relationship and end needless conflicts. Stan Tatkin is one of the most innovative thinkers in the couples relationship world today. It's impossible to read this book without learning new patterns to enhance your love."

> —Ellyn Bader, PhD, cocreator of the developmental model of couples therapy, codirector of The Couples Institute in Menlo Park, CA, and author of *Tell Me No Lies* and *In Quest of the Mythical Mate*

"Reading Stan Tatkin's book makes you want to be in therapy with him. With intense and fearless clarity, he takes you into the trenches of the combative human brain and shows you how to make love, not war."

> —Esther Perel, LMFT, author of *Mating in Captivity*

# WIRED

## *for*

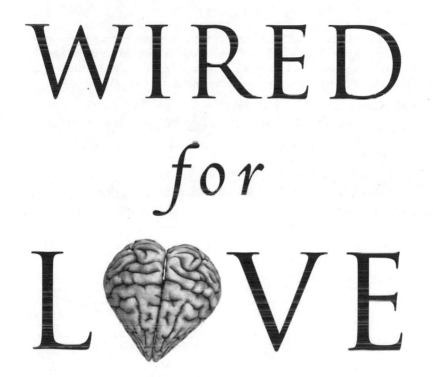

# L❤VE

## How Understanding Your Partner's Brain AND Attachment Style Can Help You Defuse Conflict AND Build a Secure Relationship

## STAN TATKIN, PSYD

NEW HARBINGER PUBLICATIONS, INC.

## Publisher's Note

Distributed in Canada by Raincoast Books

Copyright © 2011 by Stan Tatkin
New Harbinger Publications, Inc.
5674 Shattuck Avenue
Oakland, CA 94609
www.newharbinger.com

Cover design by Amy Shoup; Text design by Tracy Marie Carlson;
Acquired by Tesilya Hanauer; Edited by Clancy Drake

Library of Congress Cataloging-in-Publication Data

Tatkin, Stan.
  Wired for love : how understanding your partner's brain and attachment style can help you defuse conflict and build a secure relationship / Stan Tatkin.
    p. cm.
  Includes bibliographical references.
  ISBN 978-1-60882-058-0 (pbk.) -- ISBN 978-1-60882-059-7 (pdf e-book)
  1. Intimacy (Psychology) 2. Interpersonal relations--Psychological aspects. 3. Cognitive psychology.  I. Title.
  BF575.I5T38 2012
  158.2'4--dc23
                                    2011028010

Printed in the United States of America

16     15     14

15     14     13     12     11     10     9     8     7

*To my wife, Tracey, and daughter, Joanna,*
*who keep me going and loving life.*

# Contents

# Acknowledgments

First I must acknowledge my editor and dear friend, Jude Berman, who has kept me going and writing when my own avoidance and island nature take over. Without her guidance and gentle pressure, this book would certainly not have come to be. I have many mentors in my life to whom I am indebted: Allan Schore, Marion Solomon, Stephen Porges, Pat Ogden, Harville Hendrix, Ellyn Bader, John Bradshaw, and John Gottman, to name just a few.

# Foreword
# by Harville Hendrix

Couplehood has been, from the dawn of human history, the primary social structure of our species, giving rise to larger structures of family, community, society, culture, and civilization. But interest in helping couples improve the quality of their relationships is a very recent phenomenon. What help couples got in the past came from their families or social institutions, primarily religious ones. But given that what happens in the home determines what happens in society, and given the perennial presence of conflict and violence between partners and among groups and cultures, we can conclude that that help was not very helpful. If we operate from the logical premise that healthy couples are essential to a healthy society, and vice versa, then "helping couples" should be elevated from a romantic sentiment—and a professional career—to a primary social value. The best thing a society can do for itself is to promote and support healthy couples, and the best thing partners can do for themselves, for their children, and for society is to have a healthy relationship! This book points in that direction, describing and giving concrete guidance toward a view of intimate partnership that can help couples shift their focus from personally centered needs to the needs of their relationship and, by extension, to the transformation of society.

This radical position—that by transforming couplehood we transform every social structure—has been in the making only in the last twenty-five years or so. I want to briefly trace the emergence of couplehood—and of the evolving notions of "help" for couples—so that couples who read this splendid book can have a sense of their place in the history of this primary relationship. I want to also put *Wired for Love* in context.

We have little information about how prehistoric couples chose each other and how they related to each other, but the informed imagination of cultural anthropologist Helen Fisher offers us some clues that prior to 11,000 years ago, couples formed a "pair bond" for the purposes of procreation and physical survival. She believes this bond was based on an implicit ethic of "sharing" that served mutual interests and needs. Their roles were specific. Women gathered wood for the fires, cared for the children, and gathered fruit, berries, nuts, and roots, which they shared with the men. Men hunted wild game, which they shared with the women and children, whom they also protected from other men and wild animals. While these pair relationships were clearly sexual, they were not very durable and it is probable that they were not very intimate. Estimates are that they lasted about three years on average, or until the children were mobile. Both sexes repeatedly sought and consummated other relationships. Women gave birth to many children from different fathers and men sired many children with whom they most likely spent little time and whom they seldom recognized as their progeny. Most children were reared by single mothers and transient fathers.

That all changed about 11,000 years ago when, according to the same body of research, the hunters and gatherers learned how to grow food and corral and breed animals. No longer having to search for food, they settled down into small compounds and villages, and the concept of "property" that had to be protected arose. This concept may have applied at first only to animals and crops, but since children and women also needed protection, the concept eventually extended to include them. Small social groups evolved into villages, cities, and even empires, adding new layers of importance to social relations. The concept of property ownership gave birth to economics, and who children belonged to and whom they married became critically important components of both social and economic structures. So the second version of couplehood, the "arranged marriage," was born. It had nothing to do with romantic attraction, personal needs, or mature love and everything to do with social status, economic security, and political expedience. So parents collaborated with other parents, usually without much regard for the preferences of their sons and daughters, to select spouses for their children who would improve or maintain the social and economic status of the family as a whole. Little if any attention was paid to the quality of the couple's relationship. The couple were expected to honor family values and approved social etiquette irrespective of their feelings for each other, and if one of them transgressed—through abandonment or infidelity or other dishonorable conduct—the transgressor was advised, admonished, and/or punished by family and community leaders—father, brothers, elders, religious officials. The tools of analysis, understanding, and empathy had not yet been invented.

The next incarnation of marriage began in the eighteenth century with the rise in Europe of democratic political institutions, which argued that everyone was entitled to personal freedom—and, by extension, the freedom to marry the person of their choice. The door to marriage was, increasingly, romantic love rather than parental dictates, and this shift gave rise to the personal or psychological marriage designed to meet personal and psychological rather than social and economic needs. However, until Sigmund Freud's discovery of the unconscious and founding of psychotherapy at the end of the nineteenth century, it was little guessed that our unconscious minds are deeply involved in our personal choices and that our past interpersonal experiences have a powerful impact on our present adult relationships. The discovery that this was so led to the awareness that our choice of a partner, if it is romantic, is influenced by our unconscious minds more than our rational preferences. The partner we unconsciously choose is dauntingly similar—warts and all, and especially the warts—to the caretakers who reared us. Thus the needs we want met in our adult intimate relationship—those that were not met in childhood—are presented to persons who are woefully similar to the persons who did not meet those needs when we were children. The dissatisfaction arising from this cruel incompatibility eventually contributed to a rise in the divorce rate. While divorce was essentially forbidden in the arranged marriage and profoundly discouraged in the romantic marriage until recently, the rising divorce rate, especially after the post–World War II population explosion in the 1950s, gave birth to marriage counseling and marital therapy as professions. Help for couples was expanded from traditional (religious, familial) sources to an emerging mental health profession whose members had varying degrees of training and competence.

The early models of marriage counseling were based upon the assumption that a couple consisted of two independent, autonomous persons who could use their learning capacity and cognitive skills to resolve their differences by regulating conflict about their differences. This assumption shifted help from advice, instruction, and admonition—the method of parents and religious professionals before the development of professional counseling and psychotherapy—to conflict resolution, negotiation, and problem solving. This was helpful to some couples whose issues were not so difficult, but for others the conflict resolution process was a failure. These more difficult couples were advised to engage in depth psychotherapy to work through their long-standing personal problems independent of their relationship, and to separate from each other with the assumption that when they came back together, free of their personal neuroses, they could meet each others' needs, current and past, and create a satisfying and wonderful relationship.

This model did not work very well. Most partners who were successful in their private psychotherapy tended to divorce rather than reconcile. The divorce rate reached about 50 percent, and there it has held steady for the past sixty years. The statistics on the success of marriage therapy has held steady at around 30 percent—not a shining success for this fledgling profession.

In recent years we have discovered that the major problem with this model is its focus on the "individual" as the foundational unit of society and on the satisfaction of personal needs as the goal of marriage. Given that democracy gave political reality to the concept of the individual and Freud illuminated the architecture of the interior of the self, this perspective makes sense. It led Freud to locate the human problem inside the individual and to create psychotherapy as a cure for the ills of the self. Since marital counseling and couples therapy are the handmaidens of psychotherapy, it makes sense that marital therapy would focus on healing the individuals as a precondition for a satisfying relationship. It also makes sense that therapists would assume that the problem was unmet needs "inside" the individuals and that relationships existed to satisfy those needs. This all give birth to this narrative of marriage: If your relationship is not satisfying your needs, you are married to the wrong person. You have a right to the satisfaction of your needs in a relationship, and if that does not happen, you should change partners and try again to get the same needs met with a different person. To put it in more crass terms, your marriage is about "you" and your needs and if it does not provide you with satisfaction, its dissolution is justifiable no matter the consequences for others, even the children.

This narrative has birthed the phenomena of multiple marriages, one-parent families, shattered children, the "starter" marriage, and cohabitation as a substitute for marriage, as well as a trend toward tying the knot at later and later ages. Since, as was stated above, a society reflects the quality of couples' relationships, this focus on the self has also mirrored and fed a society of abuse and violence ranging from endemic negativity to domestic abuse, addictions of all kinds, crime, poverty, and war. These huge social issues cannot be changed until a different narrative about how to be in an intimate relationship emerges.

I believe a new narrative that shifts the focus from the self and personal need satisfaction to the relationship began to emerge in the last quarter of the twentieth century. In the seventies, a new view of the self as intrinsically relational and interdependent began to challenge the reigning view of the self as autonomous, independent, and self-sufficient. This paradigm shift was fomented by developmental psychologists who began to describe the newborn child as "social" at birth rather than becoming social at a later developmental stage. Humans beings, they began to say, are inherently relational and relationally dependent. At the same time, other students of the child-parent relationship began to say that there is no such thing as an "individual," there is only a mother-child relationship, thus making relationship foundational rather than the individual. The isolated and autonomous self was exposed as a myth. The origin of the human problem was relocated from the interior of the self to the failure of relationship "between" caretakers and their infant children. These failed relationships, the new researchers said, are the source of suffering in the interior soul, and its relief requires participation in a relationship that is the antithesis of the early parent-child drama. Since these students of the human situation tended to be therapists, they assumed the optimal corrective relationship was with a therapist.

In the past twenty years, these insights have become the theme of a new marital narrative and the fourth incarnation of marriage, which I refer to as the "conscious partnership." In this new narrative, commitment is to the needs of the relationship rather than to the needs of the self. It goes something like this: Your marriage is not about you. Your marriage is about itself; it is a third reality to which and for which you are responsible, and only by honoring that responsibility will you get your childhood and current needs met. When you make your relationship primary and your needs secondary, you produce the paradoxical effect of getting your needs met in ways they can never be met if you make them primary. What happens is not so much the healing of childhood wounds, which may in fact not be healable, but the creation of a relationship in which two persons are reliably and sustainably present to each other empathically. This new emotional environment develops new neural pathways flowered with loving presence that replace the old toxic pathways that are filled with the debris of the sufferings of childhood. Couplehood becomes the container for the joy of being, which is a connected relationship. And, since the quality of couplehood determines the tenor of the social fabric, the extension of that joy from the local to the global could heal most human suffering.

In my view, *Wired for Love* by Stan Tatkin is more than an addition to the vast literature directed to couples. It is more than a brilliant integration of recent brain research with the insights of attachment theory. It is an instance of an emergent literature expressing a new paradigm of couplehood. This is no small achievement: this book will help couples flourish in their relationships and it will aid the professionals who want to help couples be more effective. Since the author has provided a thorough guide for those on the journey to lasting love, it requires no summary here. It speaks for itself, and I encourage you to begin reading now. Your view of how to be in an intimate relationship and of the potential of marriage for personal and social healing will change forever!

# Introduction: Wired for Love

Look around you. We live in a highly complex world. The array of devices, machinery, technology, and processes that make it tick is mindboggling. Just within the lifetime of many still alive today, humanity has come to regard as commonplace travel to the far side of the planet, the instant replay of events around the globe, and the ability to speak to and see just about anyone anywhere at any time, among many other things. We enjoy the advantages these scientific advances have brought us, and we curse them when they break down. And of course they do break down at times. For this reason, we turn to guidebooks—everything from a car owner's manual that shows how much to inflate your tires, to the instructions that show how much batter to load in your waffle maker. We may hate the thought of consulting a manual (or calling for technical support, except perhaps in a pinch), but can you really operate all these things successfully simply through intuition?

Relationships are complex, too. Yet we often attempt them with a minimum of guidance and support. I'm not suggesting you should follow a standard set of 1-2-3 steps in relating to your partner. Relationships will never come with manuals that automate the process. We aren't robots. What works for one couple won't necessarily work for another. But neither does it work to fly blind, as many couples do, and expect relationships to fall into place.

Hence the need for well-informed guidance that supports your relationship.

And what might be considered well-informed in this context? In fact, a large and fascinating body of scientific knowledge and theory with the potential to influence how partners relate to one another has been accruing in recent decades. This includes revolutionary work in the fields of neuroscience and neurobiology, psychophysiology, and psychology. I believe couples can benefit from this wealth of research. You may find this idea intimidating, but don't worry: I'm not suggesting you need to quit your day job and go back to school. I think you'll find the basic theories quite straightforward when you hear them explained in lay language.

In short, it's my conviction that having a better understanding about how our brains function—in other words, how we're wired—puts us in a better position to make well-informed choices in our relationships. Scientific evidence suggests that, from a biological standpoint, we humans have been wired largely for purposes that are more warlike than loving in nature. That's the bad news. But the good news is that recent research suggests a variety of strategies and techniques are available to reverse this predisposition. We can, in effect, take steps to assure we are primarily wired for love. These strategies can help us create stable, loving relationships in which we are poised to effectively defuse conflict when it arises.

So why not make use of them? In the first three chapters of this book, I provide you with general principles, drawn from cutting-edge research, to help you understand what makes a relationship successful and work toward that with your partner. The chapters that follow expand on these principles in practical ways. For example, if you have a clear sense of your partner's relationship style based on the latest research, it will be easier for the two of you to work together and fix any problems that may arise. In essence, this book can serve as an owner's manual for understanding yourself, your partner, and your relationship.

Now, you may raise your eyebrows at the notion of an owner's manual. Your partner isn't property, after all. I couldn't agree more. However, I like this metaphor because it conveys the level of mutual responsibility and detailed knowledge of the relationship a couple needs to be successful. In fact, I would propose to you that all couples do in fact follow one or another set of rules and principles in their relationship. They may not be conscious of it, but they already have an owner's manual of sorts. Unfortunately, many couples have the wrong manual. And in the case of distressed couples, they *always* have it wrong.

In my work with couples, I've noticed that partners tend to form their own theories about the cause of their problems. They do this out of distress and despair, and out of their need to know why: "Why am I in pain?" "Why am I feeling threatened or unsafe?" "Why is this relationship not working out as expected?" Partners work hard to come up with answers to such questions, and sometimes their answers provide an immediate sense of relief ("Now I know why this is happening").

However, in the long run, these theories generally don't work. They aren't sufficiently accurate to help the relationship. They don't stop the pain. They don't alter our fundamental wiring. Ultimately, relying on such theories is one way of flying blind. In fact, at times, inaccurate theories further undermine a couple's sense of security and happiness. More often than not, instead of ending the war between partners, grasping onto reasons and theories only creates more of a fortress. It only supplies more ammunition for the couple to throw at one another.

I've noticed partners' theories almost always are pro-self, not pro-relationship. For instance, one partner says, "We argue because he doesn't like the same things I like." Another says, "She's so inconsiderate; no wonder I feel hurt." Or "This relationship isn't working because he's not the person I married." In each case, the focus is on the individual coming up with the theory. One of the most important discoveries a couple can make is that it is possible to shift into a pro-relationship stance. Theories from this stance sound more like the following: "We have problems sticking to our agreements," or "We do things that hurt one another." To make this shift, partners must be willing to throw out their old theories and consider new ones. They must be willing to rewire.

Personally, I learned some of this the hard way.

For many years, my specialty as a psychotherapist was working with individuals suffering from personality disorders. I became interested in the early prevention of such disorders. As my practice began to focus more on adult couples, I found myself wanting to identify, earlier in the therapy, ways to prevent their problems, too.

Around this time, one of the great shocks of my life came to pass. My first wife and I divorced. During the period that followed, my need to understand why my marriage had failed led to a creative obsession, spurring me to more closely investigate the science behind relationships. I sensed that my fellow therapists and I must be missing something, something more we could do to help couples in distress. And could do earlier in their relationship. I might not have been able to salvage my marriage, but I could try harder to prevent failure for others…and for myself in the future.

Ultimately, I came up with several key areas of research I believed could point toward the difference between success and failure in relationships. I'm not speaking of research I conducted; these were the fields of study I mentioned earlier that have witnessed enormous leaps forward in the past few decades. The more I studied the latest findings and observed how they played out daily in my office, the more lights flashed in my mind. I realized this valuable knowledge wasn't being properly synthesized for and focused on adult couples. Therapists working with couples had not begun to connect the disparate dots of various sciences. They were a bit like technical support people working with out-of-date manuals. Their advice only went so far. I became convinced the most important thing I could do with my time and energy was to find the connections between these areas of research and put them to practical clinical use.

One of these areas is the field of neuroscience, the study of the human brain. This, I discovered, provides a physiological basis for understanding our strengths and weaknesses, including those that drive our relationships. For example, I am utterly stupid when it comes to math, an ability managed by many parts of the brain, such as the intraparietal sulcus. Fortunately, my work doesn't depend on math, nor do my relationships with my wife and daughter. But my ability to read faces, emotional tone, and social cues (managed by the brain's right hemisphere) is a different matter. If I were weak in that area, I would be out of a job and maybe even a marriage (again). As we will see in chapter 2, some parts of our brain predispose us to first and foremost seek security. This can wreak havoc on a relationship if we don't learn to use the more evolved parts of the brain to override this wiring and exert control over the primitive parts.

A second area of research is attachment theory, which explains our biological need to attach to or bond with others, starting with our earliest relationships. Our early experiences form an instructional blueprint that is stored in body memory and becomes part of our basic relational wiring—our sense of safety and security. In a nutshell, some individuals are fundamentally secure in their relationships, while others are insecure. Insecurity can lead us to remain distant from a partner or to harbor ambivalence about relating. However insecurity manifests, as we will see in chapter 3, it has insidious effects on a relationship if we don't try to rewire the dysfunctional tendencies acquired early in life.

The third area of research I found fascinating and helpful was the biology of human arousal. When you hear of arousal, you may immediately think of sexual arousal. But I am referring here to a more general sense of arousal: our moment-to-moment ability to manage our energy, alertness, and readiness to engage. In the context of couples, research in this area suggests how we as partners can manage one another's highs and lows. We don't have to remain at the mercy of each other's runaway moods and feelings. Rather, as competent managers of our partners, we can become expert at moving, shifting, motivating, influencing, soothing, and inspiring one another.

Each of these areas of research informs this book. In the past ten years, I have synthesized these ideas and integrated them into my therapy practice. I call this work a *psychobiological* approach. Along the way, I realized this approach isn't of value just to couples seeking therapy; everyone who is in or is planning to be in, or even hoping to be in, a relationship can benefit.

And I have been a prime beneficiary. All the hard work I did paved the way for my current marriage, in which I discovered, and have for the first time been able to enjoy, a secure, functioning family. This relationship became the gold standard by which I could test and measure the principles described in this book.

As I mentioned, many couples seek reasons for their problems. Yet the theories and reasons they come up with generally are false. The approach I am offering can, I believe, make the difference. In a nutshell, I'll help you harness the power of your brain and your partner's brain for love instead of war, in a scientifically supported way. In this book, I present ten key principles that show you how to avoid common pitfalls that deter or undermine so many relationships. These principles are:

♥ Creating a couple bubble allows partners to keep each other safe and secure.

♥ Partners can make love and avoid war when the security-seeking parts of the brain are put at ease.

♥ Partners relate to one another primarily as anchors (securely attached), islands (insecurely avoidant), or waves (insecurely ambivalent).

♥    Partners who are experts on one another know how to please and soothe each other.

♥    Partners with busy lives should create and use bedtime and morning rituals, as well as reunion rituals, to stay connected.

♥    Partners should serve as the primary go-to people for one another.

♥    Partners should prevent each other from being a third wheel when relating to outsiders.

♥    Partners who want to stay together must learn to fight well.

♥    Partners can rekindle their love at any time through eye contact.

♥    Partners can minimize each other's stress and optimize each other's health.

These principles are based on the latest science, but let me stress again: you don't have to grasp the technicalities of the science to understand these principles. I have done that for you. In fact, I've done my best to make them fun and enjoyable. I promise not to put you to sleep with scientific jargon. As I said, life is complex enough already. If there is a hallmark for this age, perhaps it will be our ability to take the complex findings of scientific research and apply them smoothly and effectively in our everyday lives, to better understand ourselves and to love more fully.

Each chapter includes exercises to help you apply the principle discussed therein. You can do most of the exercises on your own, or you and your partner can do them together. Actually, there is a certain irony here. An important premise of this book is that happy couples share a high degree of closeness and togetherness. Yet most people tend to read books—even books about relationships—on their own. So I encourage you to buck this trend. Share what is in this book with your partner. You will get even more out of it.

# CHAPTER 1

# The Couple Bubble: How You Can Keep Each Other Safe and Secure

Who among us doesn't want to feel loved? Finally to be able to be ourselves just as we are, to feel cherished, cared for, and protected—this has been the pursuit of humans since the beginning of recorded time. We are social animals. We depend on other people. We need other people.

Some of us have parents or siblings or cousins or other family members to give us respite. Some of us turn to friends or colleagues. Some of us turn to drugs and alcohol or other substances or activities that make us feel alive, wanted, satisfied, relieved, or calmed. Some of us turn to personal growth seminars, or even seek psychological treatment. Some of us turn to our work or focus on hobbies. One way or another—through wholesome, healthy means or less-than-savory means—we seek our safe zone.

This longing for a safe zone is one reason we pair up. However, partners—whether in a romantic relationship or committed friendship—often fail to use each other as advocates and allies against all hostile forces. They don't see the opportunities to make a home for one another; to create a safe place in which to relax and feel accepted, wanted, protected, and cared for. I see this frequently in couples who seek therapy. Often it is the very reason they seek professional help.

# The Relationship Comes First

Jenny and Bradley were on the brink of break-up. Neither wanted to end the relationship, but bad things kept happening, and each blamed the other. They had started dating as freshmen, and they were now about to graduate from college. Both wanted to get married and have a family.

Jenny's family resided on the East Coast near the college. She enjoyed close ties with them, particularly her mother, with whom she spoke daily. Bradley hailed from the West Coast, where his family lived. Because of the distance, he made only one trip annually, each time inviting Jenny. She often felt neglected during these trips, despite the fact that she adored Bradley's father. Bradley liked to attend parties and engage with his friends in a way that left Jenny to fend alone against advances from other men and what she considered dull conversations with their dates. Bradley never seemed to notice Jenny's discontent during these events, but certainly felt the sting of her angry withdrawal afterward.

Their conversations would go something like this:

"You always do this!" she says. "You bring me to these things and then leave me standing there as if I don't exist. I don't know why you bother to invite me!"

Bradley's response is defensive. "I'm sick and tired of having this conversation. You're being ridiculous. I didn't do anything wrong!"

To make her case, Jenny brings up Bradley's friend, Tommy, who she says has been inappropriate with her. "He gets drunk and comes on to me, and you don't even notice. I don't feel protected by you at all."

Bradley's response, again, is dismissive. "He's just playing around."

These conversations usually ended with Jenny going off to sulk and Bradley feeling punished. Nor did things go better when the situation was reversed. Jenny often visited her family, and expected Bradley to join her. He complained she disappeared with her mother and sisters, forcing him to "hang" with her father, with whom he had little in common. When the couple were alone, their conversations about this sounded similar in many ways to the previous one:

"I can't stand coming here," Bradley complains.

"Why?" Jenny sounds surprised.

"You keep sticking me with your father. I feel like a worm because he thinks I'm not good enough for you, and at dinner you act like you agree with him!" Bradley's voice rises in anger.

"Shhh," Jenny replies. "Don't yell."

Bradley stops himself, pursing his lips and dropping his head. "I don't get it," he says in a lowered voice.

"Get what?"

"Why you invite me. I just feel bad here," he says, without raising his head to look at her.

Jenny softens and moves toward him with a loving gesture. "My family loves you," she says. "I hear that all the time from Mom and my sisters. Dad likes you, too, he's just…like that."

Bradley's face snaps into view, reddened, with tears in his eyes. "That's baloney! If your family 'loves me,'" he says with finger quotations, "why don't I hear it from them? If your dad is so loving, why don't *you* sit with him, and let me hang with your mom?"

"Now you're being ridiculous," Jenny replies as she heads for the door. "Just forget it!"

"And you know what else?" Bradley continues in hopes of her hearing. "You're just like your dad. You put me down right in front of everyone."

Jenny leaves the room, slamming the door behind her.

When we enter into a relationship, we want to matter to our partner, to be visible and important. As in the case of Jenny and Bradley, we may not know how to achieve this, but we want it so much that it shapes much of what we do and say to one another. We want to know our efforts are noticed and appreciated. We want to know our relationship is regarded as important by our partner and will not be relegated to second or third place because of a competing person, task, or thing.

It hasn't always been this way. If we compare today's love relationships with the relationships of old, we might be gravely disappointed. In centuries past, rarely did couples get together simply because they loved one another. Marriages were arranged for political, religious, and economic purposes. Husbands and wives stayed together to provide security for their family. At the same time, duty and obligation—for both partners—served a male-advantaged social contract. Safety and security came at an emotional price. Yet no one complained, because nobody expected anything different.

In our modern Western culture, marriage for love tends to be the norm. We expect to be swept off our feet or to feel whole and completed or to believe we've met our soul mate. And we expect this profound connection to sustain our relationship. Nothing seems more important. However, these feelings and ideals often exact a price if we as partners are unable to provide one another with a satisfying level of security. The truth is, even if a couple does experience a profound connection, this represents only the beginning of their relationship. What ultimately counts in the life of the couple is what happens after their courtship, love affair, or infatuation phase. What counts is their ability to be there for one another, no matter what.

Consider another couple, Greta and Bram, both thirty. When they married a year ago, they rented an apartment in the city, where Greta was securely employed as a school teacher. Bram's family lived in a nearby rural town, and he commuted to work in the family agricultural business.

Each year, Greta was required to attend a gala fundraiser for her school. It was not the type of event that ordinarily suited Bram, who preferred dungarees to dress shirts, ties, and jackets. He also tended to feel shy and even a bit tongue tied, especially in gatherings with folks he didn't know. Greta, on the other hand, moved well in large circles of strangers. Despite their differences, however, Bram prepared himself for an evening with Greta on his arm.

Their conversation as they dressed went something like this:

"It's not you, you know," Bram says with a concerned look on his face, while on his third attempt to make a proper tie. "I just don't like being with all these people I don't know."

"I know," Greta replies, staring straight ahead as she applies her eyeliner. "I appreciate your willingness to come anyway. The moment you want to leave, we'll go. Okay?"

"Okay," says Bram, as he finally gets the tie right.

After she parks their car, Greta turns to Bram and switches on the overhead light. "How do I look?" she asks, puckering her lips.

"Beautiful as usual," Bram replies with a lingering gaze into her eyes.

She scans his eyes in return, and a moment passes as they enjoy a mutual gale of excitement. "Let's make a plan," she says softly. "You'll keep me on your arm when we go in, and I'll probably see some people I know. Don't leave me, okay? I want to introduce you."

"Okay," Bram responds with an anxious smile. "What if I have to go to the bathroom?" he quips.

"You may go without me," Greta quickly responds in kind, "but after that, I expect you to get your handsome butt back to your beautiful wife."

They share a smile and kiss. "This job is important," Greta says as they get out of the car, "but not as important as you are to me."

As you can see, Jenny and Bradley and Greta and Bram have very different ways of handling situations as a couple. It's probably obvious which relationship works better, feels better, and deserves to be held up as exemplary. But let's look at both couples in greater detail and see if we can understand why they function as they do, and how they came to be as they are.

# Autonomy versus Mutuality

Implicit in Jenny's and Bradley's narrative is a belief that each should stand independent of the other and should not expect to be looked after. We could say their model is one of autonomy. That is, they see themselves as individuals first, and as a couple second. When push comes to shove, they prioritize their personal needs over their needs as a couple. If you questioned them about this, they might reply that they value their independence, or that they are "their own person" and don't let the other one boss them around.

However, it's not quite that simple. Yes, each expects the other to behave in an autonomous fashion, but in reality, this is the case only when it suits his or her own purpose. When either finds that the proverbial shoe is now on the other foot, he or she feels dismissed, dropped, and unimportant. This couple's sense of independence works especially poorly in situations in which they depend on one another to feel important and protected. They are unaware of this problem when they think they're maintaining their so-called autonomy, but painfully aware when they feel they are the victim of neglect.

I think it's fair to say the autonomy implied by Jenny's and Bradley's behavior is not really autonomy at all. Rather, they are living according to an "If it's good for me, you should be all right with it" type of agreement. As a result, they continually play out situations wherein they each fail to remember the other person. Their underlying message is "You do your thing and I'll do my thing." Sounds mutual, doesn't it? Yet it is anything but mutual because it requires that the other partner be okay *or else*, and it condones the partners readily throwing one another under the bus. This brand of autonomy doesn't reflect true independence, but rather a fear of dependency. Instead of representing strength, it can represent weakness.

In contrast, Bram and Greta each appear to know something about how the other thinks and feels, and each cares about that. We can say their model is one of mutuality. It is based on sharing and mutual respect. Neither expects the other to be different from who he or she is, and both use this shared knowledge as a way to protect one another in private as well as public settings. For example, Greta anticipates Bram's discomfort and addresses it in a way that protects his dignity. She acts as if she needs him, though she knows he is the needier one in this situation. Neither Bram nor Greta is poised to throw the other under the bus. It is as if they maintain a protective bubble around themselves.

The *couple bubble* is a term I like to use to describe the mutually constructed membrane, cocoon, or womb that holds a couple together and protects each partner from outside elements. A couple bubble is an intimate environment that the partners create and sustain together and that implicitly guarantees such things as:

- ♥ "I will never leave you."

- ♥ "I will never frighten you purposely."

- ♥ "When you are in distress, I will relieve you, even if I'm the one who is causing the distress."

- ♥ "Our relationship is more important than my need to be right, your performance, your appearance, what other people think or want, or any other competing value."

- ♥ "You will be the first to hear about anything and not the second, third, or fourth person I tell."

I say "implicitly," but couples can and often do make explicit agreements around any or all of the elements that constitute the couple bubble.

---

## EXERCISE: HOW CLOSE ARE YOU?

The feeling of closeness is subjective; that is, how close you feel to your partner and how safe you feel both take place within you. You may feel very close to your partner, but he or she isn't likely to know how you feel unless you say so. And the same goes for how your partner feels about you.

Now, discover some of the ways you offer closeness to your partner.

1. In the previous section, I listed some guarantees couples give one another—for example, saying, "I will never leave you." What such guarantees have you given to your partner?

2. What guarantees would you like to give?

3. What guarantees would you like to receive?

4. You don't need to receive a guarantee from your partner before you offer one. Look for moments when you can express your feelings of closeness and promise safety.

---

# HOW COUPLES COME TO VALUE AUTONOMY OVER MUTUALITY

Alongside our modern Western emphasis on autonomy, we see increasing evidence of loneliness inside and outside of marriages; a rising incidence of violence and alienation; and divorce rates that, while they may be decreasing, remain well above ideal. Like Jenny and Bradley, couples in distress too often turn to solutions that can be summed up by "You do your thing and I'll do my thing" or "You take care of yourself and I'll take care of myself." We hear pop psychology pronouncements such as "I'm not ready to be in a relationship" and "You have to love yourself before anyone can love you."

Is any of this true? Is it really possible to love yourself before someone ever loves you?

Think about it. How could this be true? If it were true, babies would come into this world already self-loving or self-hating. And we know they don't. In fact, human beings don't start by thinking anything about themselves, good or bad. We learn to love ourselves precisely *because* we have experienced being loved by someone. We learn to take care of ourselves because somebody has taken care of us. Our self-worth and self-esteem also develop because of other people.

If you don't agree with what I'm suggesting, check it out for yourself. Think of a time when you were young and your parents didn't believe in you in some way. Were you still able to believe in yourself? Maybe you were. But if so, how did you do it? From where or from whom did you get your belief? Or think of an ex–romantic partner who didn't believe in you or trust you. Were you able to believe in or trust yourself nonetheless? From where did you get that belief and trust? In each of these cases, chances are very good that if you did believe in yourself, that belief originated with somebody important to you. This is how we come to be as we are: all our prior interactions and relationships have shaped the person we are today.

Many couples who come together these days share various ideals about love relationships, yet their prior experiences of love don't match up with their ideals. That's a problem, because nitty-gritty personal history always trumps ideals. This is just the way we're wired. If, for example, we didn't witness devotion in our parents' marriage, we won't have positive role models for loving to draw upon in our own adult relationships. If we never saw mutual care, sensitivity, and repair in our parents' marriage, those values likely will elude us.

Our two couples clearly illustrate this principle. Neither Bradley nor Jenny is doing anything radically different from what he or she experienced as a child. For instance, Jenny's mother often abandoned Jenny's father in social situations, just as Jenny now abandons Bradley. Jenny never experienced her parents as loving or close. To the contrary, they often used the children in their arguments. Jenny's mother complained to her father about his going off to be with his pals at the bar and leaving her to fend for herself. Bradley's parents often were too busy doing their own thing to spend much time with their kids. His mother was known to drive his father out of the house with her criticism, something Bradley also resents whenever he becomes Jenny's target of harsh judgment.

Neither Bram nor Greta consider their parents perfect, but both felt as children that their parents loved and respected one another. Both have childhood memories of their parents apologizing to one another and fixing without much delay any hurt feelings that arose between them. Greta's mother was quite skilled at handling Greta's father, who sometimes got rather grumpy and difficult. Because she had learned from her mother how to respond to him—in the best way, mind you—Greta was never afraid to approach her father. Despite his irascible nature, she knew her father was devoted to her mother's happiness and well-being.

Bram had a similar experience, though in reverse. His mother was high strung, which sometimes caused problems outside the home. His father, on the other hand, was rather low-key and had no difficulty responding to his mother in the best way. Bram's father loved his mother's liveliness and spunkiness; his mother loved the father's calmness and unflappability. When I speak about responding to a partner "in the best way," I mean in a way that works well for and feels good to both individuals.

## WHY PAIR UP?

You might be wondering whether the kind of commitment I'm suggesting is one you want to make. In fact, this raises the question, why pair up at all?

There is nothing inherently better about coupling than about being single. This book is not about which is better, a single lifestyle or a coupled lifestyle. I know plenty of perfectly happy singles who neither feel the need to avoid coupling nor weep about being uncoupled. These individuals are fine with their lives either way: if a relationship happens to develop, that would be great, and if not, that would be dandy as well. Moreover, research on the relative merits of relationships has failed to yield firm conclusions one way or the other. Some data—including statistics popularized by authors Linda Waite and Maggie Gallagher in their book *The Case for Marriage* (2000)—suggest that married people are happier and healthier than are nonmarried people. However, others—including Alois Stutzer and Bruno Frey (2003) in Germany and Richard Lucas and Andrew Clark (2006) in the US—have reported that people who get married tend to be happier in the first place than people who don't marry. Janice Kiecolt-Glaser and her colleagues (2005) found unhappily married folks to be more prone to illness than are happily single folks.

One obvious reason people pair up is for procreation. This instinct is embedded in our DNA to ensure the survival of our species. However, pairing up for this purpose doesn't necessarily translate into the need for a long-term, committed relationship. There's certainly no proof, at least as far as our species is concerned, that monogamy is nature's mandate. I find it interesting that some mammals, such as wolves and prairie voles, do pair up for life. In fact, neurobiologists studying voles report that prairie voles (who bond with a partner for life) and meadow voles (who do not bond for life) have identifiable genetic differences. It is possible scientists one day will identify human genes that explain why we do or don't decide to pair up.

In the meantime, to understand the purpose of pairing up with another human being, we can think about what happens to a baby. Ideally, all babies have a parent or other caregiver who puts their relationship before all other matters. The baby feels loved and secure, and the adult also enjoys the feeling of being loved and of being with and caring for the baby. The two are in it together. We call this a *primary attachment relationship,* because the baby and caregiver are bonded, or attached, to one another. You could say this is a "baby bubble"—much like the couple bubble, only occurring during infancy.

This baby bubble sets the stage for enjoyable relationships with others later in life. If at an early age we experienced security and a love we could trust, we carry this with us. As adults, we are able to form new primary attachment relationships. We feel capable of being strong and loving and secure. On the other hand, if at an early age our relationships with caregivers were less than secure, and the caregiver did not seem to value being with us over all other matters, we are likely to be fearful or worried about entering into or being in relationships. (We will talk in more depth about attachment in the next chapter.)

## WE COME FIRST

Obviously we can't change what happened when we were infants. However, if those early influences are affecting how we feel about relationships now, if they hinder our ability to form the kinds of bonds we want in our lives now, we can work toward resolving them. For some couples, therapy is helpful to achieve this kind of rewiring. Other couples are able to discuss and work on their issues together, with minimal external input.

Let's look at what it takes to create a couple bubble in which you as partners keep one another safe and secure.

## MAKING THE PACT

The couple bubble is an agreement to put the relationship before anything and everything else. It means putting your partner's well-being, self-esteem, and distress relief first. And it means your partner does the same for you. You both agree to do it for each other. Therefore, you say to each other, "*We* come first." In this way, you cement your relationship. It is like making a pact or taking a vow, or like reinforcing a vow you already took with one another.

Sometimes people say, "I don't want to commit until I can be sure this thing that worries me about you won't be a problem." I have heard variations of this from both men and women in my years as a couples therapist. Popular deal breakers include religion, money, kids, time, and sexuality. There's no better way to scare off a potential partner than to suggest he or she is inadequate with respect to any of these, or to insist that partner prove himself or herself before security is assured. This kind of approach is doomed to failure.

Partners entering into a couple bubble agreement have to buy into it and own it to fully appreciate it. They have to be in all the way. When partners don't honor the couple bubble and complain they aren't being well cared for, often the reason is that they get exactly what they paid for. Pay for part of something, and you get part of something. Now, you might argue, "Stan, how can you say I must buy him or her in order to know whether he or she is good enough?" My answer is that if he or she is so far from good enough, then he or she shouldn't even be a contender. However, this isn't usually the case. Mostly, I see partners who have carefully and thoughtfully chosen one another, but fear the problems that arise after getting to know one another better will become deal breakers. Typically, these problems involve the positive features each chose in the other person, which they now realize also contain annoying elements. For example, you may adore his sense of humor, but now dislike that he cracks jokes when you want him to be serious. Or you may admire her musical talent, but be annoyed when she wants to practice the piano instead of walk with you.

Sometimes partners in this situation want to bargain: "Can I just take you with the parts I like, and we'll agree to hold the rest?"

Sorry. This isn't a burger joint, where you get to hold the pickles and lettuce. You want it and you buy it as is, or you move on. I realize this might sound harsh. But I have said as much to couples. And generally they respond by taking stock of the situation. They recognize the toll their ambivalence is taking on the relationship. Then they are able to move clearly in one direction or the other.

## ARE WE READY?

I'm not suggesting you try to create a couple bubble prematurely. Sometimes couples find a bubble has been created at the very start of their relationship, with no effort on their parts. A good example of this occurs in *West Side Story* when the star-crossed lovers, Tony and Maria, arrive at the dance. Their newly discovered love is represented as a spotlight on them, while everyone else fades into the background. Of course, we'll never know what would have happened if tragedy hadn't cut short their love affair. Chances are they would have had to work to maintain their couple bubble.

It is important to remember that the casual dating and courtship phases are different from a relationship that's moving toward or has become imbued with a sense of permanence. In the beginning of a relationship, we are besotted and captivated by the blissful hopefulness and mutual admiration we feel. Our brains are awash in *dopamine* and *noradrenaline*, two chemicals that greatly enhance excitement, focus, and attention. When we leave each other's orbit, our brains wrestle with diminished *serotonin*, a chemical that often calms anxiety and obsession. We find ourselves thinking, "When will I see him again?" or "Should I call her tomorrow?" and other thoughts that keep us connected to this one among billions of fishies in the social sea.

Of course, this shared lovefest obscures the fact that we don't really yet know each other well. In the moment, who cares, right? We are a bit like a rocket that is launched with sufficient acceleration to make it to the edge of

outer space, but would have to jettison its booster and engage a more enduring accelerant to go farther. In a new relationship, we're just excited to be
aiming for the stars, and assume we'll figure everything out when we get
there. But if we want the relationship to stand a chance of reaching its destination, this is precisely when we need to figure it out.

# HOLDING TO IT

The couple bubble is a pact between partners in which the quid pro quo
is to burden one another with the tasks of devotion and caring for the other's
safety, security, and well-being. This mutual burden determines the degree of
shared gratitude and valuation you both can experience. If you think about it,
when the going gets tough, the couple bubble is all you can really count on to
hold your relationship together.

This doesn't mean you won't make mistakes along the way or accidentally
hurt each other. It doesn't mean you can never make a decision that puts
yourself before the relationship, nor that you absolutely never should. These
things will happen, no matter what. However, it does mean you will hold each
other to your fundamental agreement: "We come first."

Then, when either one of you makes a mistake, the other will give a
gentle reminder: "Hey, I thought this is what we agreed to do for each other."
The transgressing partner can say, "Oh yeah, my bad," and quickly fix the
situation.

---

# EXERCISE: THE BUBBLE TROUBLE METER

After you and your partner have entered into a couple bubble agreement, the
next step is to monitor it. Although an agreement has been made, maintaining
the bubble is a process. It's ongoing. You could say the bubble assumes a life
of its own. And as such, you should periodically take its pulse.

In this exercise, you will develop a bubble trouble meter. By that I mean
you will identify the signs that tell you your couple bubble is not providing the
safety and security it was designed to provide.

1. Over the next week, observe the level of closeness you feel between yourself and your partner. Of course, closeness naturally will undergo a

certain degree of ebb and flow. What you want to do is be on the lookout for times when the ebb is serious enough to warrant sounding an alarm.

2. Pay special attention to those moments of trouble. What happens? What are you feeling, and what is your partner feeling? What kinds of things do you say to each other? For example, you might notice that you go off and leave your partner alone at such times. This then is a sign for your meter.

3. Make a list of the specific signs you identify. Share these with your partner. Discuss how you can recreate your bubble, and strengthen it to prevent further stressful incidents. Remember: the bubble protects you both! It's yours, so keep it clean and polished every day.

In later chapters, we will look in more detail at how to maintain your couple bubble.

# FIRST GUIDING PRINCIPLE

The first principle of this book is that *creating a couple bubble allows partners to keep each other safe and secure.* Together, you and your partner can create and maintain your bubble. You agree do things for one another that no other person would be willing to do, at least not without getting paid. In fact—and this is important, so listen up—anyone who offers with no strings attached to do what partners must do for each other most definitely *wants* something from you (e.g., sex, money, commitment). If you're in a committed relationship and someone else seems willing to fill in for your partner, watch out! As the saying goes, there's no such thing as a free lunch.

So, the couple bubble is something you work on together. But also keep in mind that you are responsible for your end of the deal. You keep it up because you believe in the principle, not merely because your partner is or isn't willing to do the same. It works only when both partners operate on a principled level and not on the level of "You go first."

Here are some supporting principles to guide you:

1. Devote yourself to your partner's sense of safety and security and not simply to your idea about what that should be. What may make you feel safe and secure may not be what your partner requires from you. Your job is to know what matters to your partner and how to make him or her feel safe and secure.

2. Don't pop the bubble. Because the couple bubble has as its foundation a fundamental, implicit, and absolute sense of safety and security, neither of you should have to worry that the bubble is going to pop. Acting in an ambivalent manner, or taking a stance that is partly in and partly out of the relationship, undermines the security you have created. If this is allowed to persist, one or both of you will be forced into an auditioning position and you will lose all the benefits of the bubble you have so carefully constructed.

3. Make sure the bubble is mutually maintained and honored. Note, this is not codependency. *Codependent* partners live through or for each other, while ignoring their own needs and wants, thus leading to resentment and other emotional distress. In contrast, when partners form a couple bubble, both agree on the principles and comport themselves accordingly. For example, I can say my partner should be available to me whenever I need, but I must make myself available too, without expecting him or her to go first. Then, if my partner doesn't comply with our agreed-upon principles, we have some talking to do. If either of us continues to renege on our principles, one of us surely will be fired.

4. Plan to use your couple bubble. It provides a safe place in which you and your partner can always ask each other for help, rely on one another, and share your vulnerabilities. It is your primary means of support and protection. For example, whenever you and your partner go into social situations, especially ones involving difficult people, you can make a plan ahead of time that insures you will both be protected by your bubble. As Greta and Bram did, work together so you can figuratively hold hands throughout the event. By holding hands I mean remaining in contact with one another, tracking one another, and

being available at a moment's notice. Rely on eye contact, physical contact, whispering, hand signals, smoke signals—whatever! Conspire together about how you will address difficult people. Perhaps you will literally hold hands or sit next to one another in their presence. We'll further discuss how to protect your couple bubble in chapter 7. In the meantime, remember that splitting up to deal with difficult people or situations leaves you vulnerable. Together, you can be truly formidable.

# CHAPTER 2

# The Warring/Loving Brain: How You Can Keep the Love Alive

"**A** couple bubble, huh?" Shenice says to her husband as they drive home from a therapy session.

"Cool idea," he replies, focusing on his driving.

Shenice continues, "But how can we create a bubble if only one of us is interested?"

She looks, steely eyed, toward Darius, who rolls his eyes in return.

"Don't give me that look!" Shenice barks in response. "Maybe you're interested but just can't do it," she continues. "Or what if *I* can't do it? I mean, we're talking about real people with real lives."

Darius and Shenice, married seven years, with two small children, adore one another and have since high school. But despite their deep affection, together they are like firecrackers, each setting the other off, often without warning.

"Don't put that on me!" replies Darius, and this time Shenice rolls her eyes. "I'm interested," he says, "but you were correct when you said *you* can't do this bubble thing. I'm not the one who forgets all about you when we go to your folks."

"You're bringing *that* up again?" Shenice throws her head back with exasperation.

Friends and family of this couple are familiar with their hair-trigger tempers and the scenes they often create in and outside their home, alone and with others. Whenever they get this way, their words and phrases are similar, as are the memories of hurt and betrayal.

Darius and Shenice fought in earlier relationships, all the way back to their original families. In calm moments, they speak softly; their conversations are fresh, not retreads of old arguments; and their banter is more playful. They likely are nestled in their couple bubble during these moments. However, when either perceives a threat cue from the other—which could be a shift in the eyes, a pause in speech, a roll of the eyes, or a strong exhale—love turns quickly to war. Their faces fill with blood; eyes widen; voices increase in volume; vocal pitch changes; limbs stiffen; and lips begin to smack, signaling dry mouth. They no longer appear as lovers or even friends, but as predators or enemies. Gone is the playful banter, gone are mentions of goodwill and friendliness, gone is the freshness of their conversation. Instead, their talk returns to old subjects, unanswered questions about the relationship, and familiar accusations and counter-accusations.

Why does all this happen?

Darius and Shenice, like the rest of us, have brains that specialize in threat perception and threat response. Unfortunately, our biological heritage doesn't automatically guarantee a couple bubble for all. But it does provide mechanisms to deal with threats to our survival. This isn't to say the whole brain is involved in warlike behavior; in fact, only part of the brain engages in threat perception and response. Other parts help us be our most loving, kind, and friendly selves. And, yes, help us create a couple bubble.

In this chapter, we take a close look at our biological inheritance, and at what it can teach us about preventing, minimizing, and recovering from the warring situations that arise in the best and worst of relationships.

# THOU SHALL NOT GET KILLED

During courtship, partners are predisposed to anticipate their best hopes coming true. As the relationship progresses and the pair become closer and more interdependent, a couple bubble may form, and the perception of permanence may emerge. This is of course what they hope for. Yet sometimes along with security comes its opposite. Fears and expectations that date back to earlier experiences of dependency, but that didn't arise during courtship or dating, are activated as commitment to the relationship increases. As a result, partners start to anticipate the worst, not the best, from their relationship. Anticipation of the worst is not logically purposeful, nor does it necessarily surface in conscious awareness, because this type of anticipation resides in the deep and wordless part of the brain.

Much of what we do as partners is fundamentally about survival and our beastly, instinctual selves. In fact, we could say the human species has survived over millennia due to the simple imperative "Thou shall not get killed." Love and war are both conditions of our human brain. Arguably, though, the brain is wired first and foremost for war, rather than for love. Its primary function is to ensure we survive as individuals and as a species. And it is very, very good at this.

Unfortunately, the parts of our brain that are good at keeping us from being killed are also quite stupid. "Shoot first, ask questions later" is the basic credo. For instance, if you were standing on a train track and a train were speeding toward you, you probably wouldn't be wondering, "Hmm, how fast is this train moving? How many people are aboard? From where did it depart? And when will it arrive at its destination?" If you did, you likely would very soon be dead. Danger requires fast action, and the fastest-acting part of our brains doesn't care about specifics, calculations, or any other factors that are time-consuming. Its job is to keep us from getting killed. Period.

So, is the brain good at keeping us alive? Definitely. But is it bad at love? You betcha! Our brain's survival skills can be at odds with love and relationship. The things we do to keep from getting killed often are exactly the things that keep us from getting into a relationship or staying in one.

Recently, much has been written in popular psychology about the differences between female and male brains. For example, thanks to research by Bente Pakkenberg and Hans Jurgen Gundersen (1997), we know males have more brain cells at birth than do females. However, the neuroscientist Paul MacLean (1996) found the female brain tends to have more symmetry and connectivity than does the male brain. From an evolutionary standpoint, the male brain is heavily wired for reaction to threat. In *Why Zebras Don't Get Ulcers*, Robert Sapolsky (2004) reported that males are more likely to quickly spring into action when threatened, and to stay alert longer, than are females. Females, on the other hand, tend to be wired to pull in others to huddle for safety. Despite minor differences between the brains and nervous systems of men and women, as humans we all share the common drives of survival and of relationship. The fundamental mechanics of our brains are the same.

# PRIMITIVES AND AMBASSADORS

The parts of the human brain that specialize in survival have been around for a long time—actually, since the dawn of our species. I like to call these warring parts our "primitives." You can think of your primitives as your beasts within. The primitives operate without your permission. They are first in the chain of command with respect to survival reflexes, and function to trump all your other needs and wants. They are agents of war (fighting and running away) and defeat (surrendering and playing dead).

Fortunately for us, we also have a more evolved, social part of our brain. In contrast to our warring brain, this functions as our loving brain. We can legitimately say it has been wired for love. I like to think of this part of the brain as the "ambassadors." Unlike the primitives, the ambassadors interact with other brains in a refined, civilized manner. You can think of your ambassadors as your diplomats within. In reality, some of our primitives function as ambassadors at times, and some of our ambassadors have primitive functions, as well. But for our purposes in understanding couple behavior, it is useful to oversimplify a bit and view them as opposing camps. Let's look more closely.

## THE PRIMITIVES

Our primitives are naturally geared to wage war. Whether it's a little battle or a big battle, they're ready to defend us, whatever it takes. They allow us to sense, feel, and react, and tend to be the first receivers of information, both inside and outside the body. This makes them fast at identifying dangers and threats, and expedient when dealing with those dangers and threats. In fact, our primitives have all the advantages millions of years of evolution can afford, such as integration, efficiency, and speed. They were the first to arrive on the scene and will likely be the last ones standing at the end (death).

So, how exactly do the primitives operate (table 2.1)? And more importantly, how can you identify them in action in your relationship?

## TABLE 2.1 YOUR PRIMITIVES IN ACTION

| Primitive | Primary function |
|---|---|
| Amygdalae | Pick up threat signals (e.g., dangerous words and phrases; dangerous faces, voices, sounds, movements, postures, smells) |
| Hypothalamus | Releases chemicals in the brain and gives instructions to the pituitary and adrenal glands to release stress chemicals into the body; signals the need to fight, flee, or freeze |
| Pituitary and adrenal glands | Receive commands from the hypothalamus to release stress chemicals |
| Dorsal motor vagal complex (dumb vagus) | Reacts to stress or danger by extensively slowing the cardiovascular and respiratory systems |

In essence, the primitives operate according to a chain of command, similar to that used by the military. When threat or danger is perceived, a sequence of events unfolds that leads either to war or to the primitives going off alert. All this takes place within our brains and bodies, often very quickly, at a level mostly beyond our awareness. Yet if we learn to look carefully, we can detect the evidence. And once we've done that, we can think about how we might influence the process. To make the sequence easier to detect, I've defined three critical stages: Red alert! Ready the troops! All-out war.

### STAGE 1: RED ALERT!

The first line of defense among the primitives is to perceive danger and sound the alarm, loud and clear: "Watch out! Danger is present!" This is carried out by one of our most primitive structures, the *amygdalae*, almond-shaped structures in the brain. The amygdalae continually sweep the environment for signs of danger, and do so in a down-and-dirty fashion. In other words, they indiscriminately grab whatever information they find. They don't have much of a strategy, nor do they stop to analyze whether the threat is real or imminent. They just scream red alert, and assume one of the ambassadors will conduct a more careful assessment and step in to correct any errors or erroneous assumptions made by the primitives in the heat of the moment. Intelligence should always be analyzed before going to war, right? However, analysis takes time, and time is a problem when danger is afoot.

The amygdalae largely run the show between a couple when they feel threatened by one another's facial expressions, vocal inflection, sharp movements, or harmful words. Instead of two whole brains at war, it is a case of dueling amygdalae—sort of like Wild West gunfighters honing in on that twitch before reaching for their pistols. Like Darius and Shenice, partners are on constant lookout for threatening signs and signals. Specifically, the right-side amygdala picks up on dangerous facial expressions, voices, sounds, movements, and postures. The left-side amygdala picks up on dangerous words and phrases.

Consider Franklin and Leia. After dating for more than a year, Leia is frustrated by Franklin's hesitancy to ask for her hand in marriage. She is all but ready to move on and date others. While driving to dinner one evening a week after Valentine's Day, they get into a fight.

After a long period of listening to music, Leia, on the passenger side, suddenly shuts off the stereo. "Can we talk?" she asks, looking ahead.

Franklin's body stiffens as he utters, "Sure." His amygdalae have picked up the tone in her voice and the events that just occurred: the silence, the turning off of music, the question "Can we talk?" His amygdalae have grabbed onto all this in a manner not available to Franklin's full awareness, and his body prepares for something vaguely warlike.

Moments before, Leia had been contentedly listening to a song with the words "Goin' to the chapel…." The image captured her amygdalae, and she suddenly felt disturbed for no apparent reason. Her attention drifted to the previous week, when she had expected a Valentine's Day proposal. Almost before she knew what was happening, the question escaped her lips. She froze with fear, anticipating Franklin's reaction to her bringing up the dreaded subject…again. Now, even though she avoids looking at him, her amygdalae have registered the slightest hint of exhalation in the pause before his response, "Sure." Her body remembers, recognizes, and anticipates war. Although she may know it would be reasonable to check for errors in her perception, that isn't foremost in her attention.

## STAGE 2: READY THE TROOPS!

When the amygdalae have sounded an alarm, the next primitive in the chain of command jumps to attention: the *hypothalamus*. The hypothalamus is the main primitive responsible for getting our minds and bodies ready for action; it directs the *pituitary and adrenal glands* to release chemicals necessary for action. These glands are messengers and foot soldiers under the direct command of the hypothalamus.

Together, these primitives form the bulk of our stress response system, releasing substances such as the acute stress response hormones adrenaline and cortisol—into our bloodstream. The fast-acting adrenaline amps us up and gets us ready to fight or flee, while the slower-acting cortisol helps us adapt to stress by reducing inflammation and damage in our body. The continual balancing act between these chemicals feeds messages back to the hypothalamus: should we continue to fight, or is it time to withdraw the troops?

As soon as the alarm for war has been sounded, the hypothalamus gives us three options: we can fight, flee, or momentarily freeze while we decide whether to fight or flee. One way or the other, the call is made: "Ready the troops!" Just as the amygdalae sent out an alarm without questioning the accuracy of information, the hypothalamus responds to the amygdalae without questions. Again, the assumption is made that the ambassadors will come along later and clean up, as needed.

In our example of Franklin and Leia, their hypothalami gave marching orders almost simultaneously with the sounding of the first threat alarm. We can see the evidence just by looking at the couple: Franklin's muscles stiffened, preparing for a fight. Leia's body froze in fear, unsure whether she could stomach another fight (although if their past battles are any indication, she's unlikely to flee). Both their lips began to smack, activating saliva and digestive juices. Their pupils dilated, and their faces reddened with increasing blood flow. Energy and alertness increased in both partners as each readied for war.

## STAGE 3: ALL-OUT WAR!

At this stage, the primitives have the run of the place. The ambassador who was supposed to be busy in the background checking for errors has shut down—or worse, become overwhelmed by the urgency of the primitives. Often the relatively slow ambassadors are beaten to the scene by the fast-moving, chaos-producing primitives. So, for the couple, it's all-out war, and there will be no clarity until the fog has cleared. Then they'll have a chance to gather the dead and count their losses.

Couples at war have certain tell-tale behavioral signs. Some partners get very excited, while others become slow, sleepy, or even collapse. Whichever posture they take, partners at war say and do things that are decidedly unfriendly. Each time they fight, they tend to recycle the same complaints, the same examples, the same theories, and the same solutions. Of course, their battles can expand, as well—to include other people ("Even so-and-so says you're self-centered"); other moments in history ("You did the same thing when we first went out"); and other topics ("When you do that, it drives me nuts, too"). Couples often spend inordinate amounts of time debating facts and struggling to reconstruct and sequence stressful relationship events, leaving them no time or resources to sort out the real reason for their conflict. In chapter 9, we will look at how you can escape from old patterns of fighting.

For now, let's return to where we left Franklin and Leia, and see what all-out war looks like for them.

Leia takes a deep breath and launches into the dreaded topic: "Remember Valentine's Day, when you got upset with me about bringing up marriage?"

"What?" says Franklin sharply. "You're mixing that up with the scene at my mom's, days before. I said I was tired of everyone pressuring me about a proposal."

"No, I'm talking about Valentine's," Leia counters. "I asked you to give me some idea if you're ever going to…"

"Here we go again," Franklin groans. "Why do you always distort everything? I said I love you and want to marry you. I said I'll ask you. And I *will*… Oh, just forget it!"

"Don't tell me to forget it!" shouts Leia. "You didn't say anything of the kind. You just told me to shut up. And I'm not distorting anything! You ignored me that whole night."

"That's not true!" screams Franklin as he swerves to avoid a car stopped ahead.

"Watch out!" yells Leia, bracing herself against the dashboard. "You're going to kill us!"

"Don't say I was ignoring you," says Franklin, trying to appear calm. "You always do this! You can't say I ignored you and also say you loved how affectionate I was."

"When did I say that?" Leia shoots back.

"You said it that night."

"No, I didn't. You're always accusing me of doing something I didn't do."

"I can't believe this!" Franklin grips the steering wheel so tightly his hands shake.

Leia sits in silence, jaw set, arms folded. Then she says icily, "Just take me home."

Franklin violently spins the car around. "Ya' got it!" he hisses. "Just what ya' wanted."

Not every couple at war is as dramatic as Franklin and Leia. War isn't necessarily a matter of volume, harsh words, and violent movements. Partners at war can engage or disengage, loudly or quietly, rudely or politely. What determines war is the partners' experience of threat and the degree to which their primitives are in control.

## THE AFTERMATH

Fighting can be very stressful for couples, no matter how long or short their relationship may be. Often the primitives remain in charge of one or both partners for a while, after the obvious battle is over.

The day after their argument, Leia wants to talk to Franklin, to try to clear the air. Her ambassadors are ready to assert themselves. However, Franklin doesn't phone or stop by after work. She has learned that whenever they fight, he withdraws for several days. He goes home to his apartment after work and lounges around with the lights down low and his phone turned off, watching television until the wee hours. Leia doesn't know how to reach out to him, and she feels abandoned. After a few days, he will pop out of his depression and phone her again.

The primitive dictating Franklin's response is the so-called *dumb vagus*. In scientific parlance, it is known as the *dorsal motor vagal complex*, but scientists sometimes refer to it as the dumb vagus because it isn't discerning or subtle in its response to threat. If we get cut, stabbed, or otherwise physically wounded, the dumb vagus protects us by lowering our heart rate and blood pressure and signaling the hypothalamus to dump pain relievers (beta endorphins, our natural opiates) into our bloodstream. When you have blood drawn, do you become queasy or light-headed? If so, that's your dumb vagus protecting you from bleeding out. Of course, you aren't in any danger, but that overreaction is why the dumb vagus is called dumb. It also comes in handy if we are about to be eaten by a lion and can't fight or run away.

In addition to physical injury, the dumb vagus can be triggered by emotional injury and threat. It likewise responds by shutting down. Blood leaves our face, our muscles lose their tone, our ears ring, and our stomach hurts. We slump, drop, collapse, and sometimes even faint. Gone is our sense of humor, our perspective, and our life energy. We descend into a valley of darkness, where it seems no one, not even we ourselves, can hurt us. This is what happens to Franklin following a fight with Leia. High on his body's natural opiates, his depressed body and brain go into an energy-conserved state, and stay there until his ambassadors finally pull him out.

---

# EXERCISE: DISCOVER YOUR PRIMITIVES

When you become aware of the role of the primitives, you gain valuable insight into your relationship. You are actually putting neurobiology to practical use.

Here is what I suggest you try the next time you and your partner find yourselves discussing a hot issue and going a bit wild.

1. Make sure you are sitting or standing across from each other so you can observe both yourself and your partner closely.

2. See if you recognize any of the stages I just described. For example, is there evidence of a red alert? Are the troops amassing yet?

3. At some point, you may want to reread the description of the stages so you have a good sense of the specific signs for each stage. For example, these may include flushing of the skin, narrowing of the eyes, dilating of the pupils, raising of the voice, and verbal expressions of threat and anger. To an extent, these signs are universal; however, I'm sure you will find ones that are unique to you and your partner.

4. Consult table 2.1 to identify which of the primitives you have caught in action.

5. Later (when things have cooled down), talk with your partner about each other's primitives. If you feel a need to lighten things up, you can name your primitives. For example, I like to think of the amygdalae as the threat detectors and the hypothalamus as the drill sergeant. Go ahead and pick your own names. You and your partner can call your respective amygdalae Fred and Ginger if that suits you.

## THE AMBASSADORS

The ambassadors are the rational, social, and very civilized part of our brain. It's not that they're disinterested in self-survival; they're on the same page as the primitives when it comes to survival. As we already noted, whenever a threat is detected, they're the ones tasked with checking and rechecking all relevant information for accuracy. Nevertheless, given their druthers, our ambassadors would just as soon use their intelligence to sustain peace and foster social harmony and lasting relationships. By nature, they are calm, cool, and collected, and like to weigh options and plan for the future. They favor complexity and novelty, and they learn quickly.

If not for our ambassadors, we would be friendless, alone, and possibly even in prison. They allow us to be in relationships for the purpose of more than simply procreation and survival of the species. Like real ambassadors, they represent us in the world. With appropriate and skillful diplomacy, they calm fears and cool tempers, either within us or within others.

Now, I don't mean to imply that ambassadors are always better or more valuable than primitives. They're not. In some cases (as we will see in the next chapter), they can be quite obnoxious, especially when they've been hijacked by primitives. Perhaps this is why Rick Hanson, in *Buddha's Brain* (Hanson and Mendius 2009), refers to ambassadors as "wolves of love" (compared with "wolves of hate," the primitives). Nevertheless, under ordinary circumstances, namely stress-free circumstances, our ambassadors do their best to help us keep love alive.

Let's meet the ambassadors and look at how they help us not only avoid war, but maintain peace and love in relationships (table 2.2).

## TABLE 2.2   YOUR AMBASSADORS IN ACTION

| Ambassador | Primary function |
|---|---|
| Ventral vagal complex (smart vagus) | Exerts a calming effect by slowing the cardiovascular and respiratory systems (e.g., by a long, slow exhale) |
| Hippocampus | Handles short-term and long-term memory, controls anti-stress hormones, and tracks location and direction |
| Insula | Provides awareness of internal bodily cues (e.g., gut feelings), including cues associated with attachment and empathy |
| Right brain | Nonverbal and intuitive; specializes in social and emotional processing (e.g., empathy) and body awareness |
| Left brain | Verbal and logical; specializes in processing detailed information and integrating complex sounds and word meanings |
| Orbitofrontal cortex | Serves as the moral and empathic center, communicates with ambassadors and primitives alike, keeping them in check |

## KEEPING THE PEACE—THE SMART VAGUS

Fortunately, our ambassadors usually do a good job of keeping our primitives in line. Because ambassadors operate more slowly than do primitives, they are particularly successful at keeping peace in situations where time is on their side.

It so happens our dumb vagus has a younger and more intelligent sibling; namely, our *smart vagus* (aka, *ventral vagal complex*). Like its relative, the smart vagus slows us down. However, instead of overreacting and shutting us down, it enables us to hold our head above water and below the stratosphere, so to speak. Stephen Porges (1995) developed what he termed the *polyvagal theory* (*poly* meaning many) to explain how the dual aspects of our vagal system (dumb and smart) switch on and off according to the needs of the moment. He referred to this as part of our complex *social engagement system*, through which our body either helps or hinders our ability to relate to one another.

For example, taking a deep, slow breath, particularly a slow exhalation, stimulates our smart vagus. Without the ability to calm ourselves down in this manner, physical proximity with another human being would be time limited at best, and romance would be short lived.

If Leia and Franklin had taken a few deep breaths while they were in the car, they might have been able to avoid going to war. Even if their argument had erupted and things had started to get out of hand, pausing to take some deep breaths could have stopped the cycle. If either had been able to appropriately modulate his or her vocal tone and volume, they might have been able to get themselves back on a peaceful track.

Partners enjoying a couple bubble benefit from the contributions of their smart vagus and its ambassador colleagues. They are able to slow down and relax together, to soothe one another, and bond intimately. They learn what to say to one another to dispel potential threats and keep the peace. We will examine this further in Chapter 4.

## EXERCISE: HOW DO YOU SOUND?

Most of the time, we don't stop to listen to the sound our voices make as we talk to our partner. We don't pay attention to the rate of our breathing. We just run on automatic pilot. But when you slow down and engage your ambassadors, you gain a wide range of options.

Next time you and your partner are talking in a relaxed setting, experiment and play with this. See what happens when you:

1. modulate your voice (louder and softer; slower and faster);

2. whisper to one another (can you do that?);

3. take a deep breath each time before you speak;

4. ask one another which tones you like and which trigger your primitives.

## KEEPING THINGS STRAIGHT—THE HIPPOCAMPUS

A harmonious relationship is one in which the partners each know who they are, and also know who the other is. They possess a basic sense of orientation within themselves and within their relationship, and this underlies their communications. They don't unnecessarily confuse one another. And if confusion ever does arise, they are able to sort it out with relative ease. We could say both that they're good at keeping things straight and that they know how to be straight with one another.

This is accomplished by another ambassador, the *hippocampus*. Its shape resembles that of a seahorse (*hippos* is "horse" in Greek), and its function is to track important stuff, such as where we are, where we're going, what just happened, and what happened weeks and months ago. It helps us remember who we are and what we're talking about.

Our hippocampus is a key ambassador because of its role in memory, its control of antistress hormones, and its ability to encode and retrieve information about our surroundings and directions. If you've ever been to London, you may be aware that the taxicab drivers there are famous for knowing where they are and where to go. They seem to have an internal virtual map enabling them to place things in spatial memory more accurately than the average person can. In fact, researchers who studied these cabbies' brains discovered they had a hippocampus larger than that of people who don't drive for a living. Not only that, but the cabbies' hippocampi actually grew larger as they spent more time on the job (Maguire et al. 2000).

For our purposes, the hippocampus is significant because it is involved with placing relationship events in time, sequence, and context. Not only does it help us find physical locations (e.g., where to meet our partner for lunch), it also helps us encode and play back who did what, when and where, and with whom. The amygdalae are the prime culprits in disabling the hippocampus during times of war. For this reason, couples at war can be at risk for memory difficulties. Like Leia and Franklin, who argued over the events on Valentine's Day, they can get embroiled in continual struggles to reconstruct and sequence stressful relationship events, and neither partner can accurately recall who said what and when. Any attempts to establish agreement only intensify the battle. In extreme cases, this constant war can literally cause our amygdalae to grow and our hippocampus to shrink!

If Leia and Franklin's ambassadors had been functioning during their argument, one or both could have said, "Oh yeah, I remember I did say that," or "You're right, that was a difficult night we had." Instead of each trying to prove the other wrong, they could have compared notes and pieced together the relevant history. Or, for that matter, one of them could have said, "You know, those details don't really matter right now. I'm more interested in what you're feeling."

## REMAINING EMPATHIC—THE INSULA

A special nod must be given to the *insula*. This ambassador gives us the ability to pick up our own body sensations, gut feelings, and heart beat. It is responsible for our ability to attach to another person, to have an orgasm, and to feel disgust. For our purposes, the insula is a vital contributor to feeling empathy. Thus, it is an especially important ambassador in the grand scheme of love.

# STAYING CONNECTED—THE RIGHT BRAIN

Led by the social chairperson of our brain, our ambassadors are focused on keeping us connected with others, especially our partner and family members. The ambassador who takes the lead in this role is the *right hemisphere* of our brain, or more simply our *right brain*.

The right brain carries our imagination, artfulness, and overarching sense of things. It is speechless, yet elegantly communicative in other ways. A great deal of our humanity, our empathy, and our ability to connect comes from this ambassador. It is by far the expert on all things social, including reading facial expressions, vocal tones, and body language.

Had either Leia's or Franklin's right brains been fully engaged, they probably wouldn't have ended up at war in the first place. One or the other might have suggested they pull the car over and talk face-to-face and eye-to-eye, or perhaps used a well-placed touch to signal friendliness and affection.

The skillful use of vocal tone, direct eye contact, and touch are all the workings of the right brain. This ambassador is superior at picking up social cues of distress and responding to them effectively, particularly through nonverbal actions or interactions that convey friendliness and warmth. These qualities are a couple's greatest antidote to war.

## TALKING IT OUT—THE LEFT BRAIN

Nonverbal connection can go a long way toward keeping love alive. But it alone is insufficient. For this reason, our right brain has a colleague: the *left hemisphere* of our brain, or simply our *left brain*. The left brain understands the importance of detail and precision. Its ability to speak its mind is legendary. In fact, it has the gift of gab and can be quite the little chatterbox.

Had Leia's and Franklin's left brains remained engaged, either or both could have made creative and meaningful statements that, if not leading to an immediate solution, might have given them a sense of possibility, newness, and relief. Either could have avoided war by saying things such as "I realize this makes you crazy but…" or "I know we can work this out…" or "I realize this is important to you, so what if we…?" Their words would have conveyed friendliness, consideration, and thoughtfulness, potentially offsetting the influence of their primitives and allowing them to talk things out to the point of relief.

You may have heard or read in the popular press about the distinction between right-brain people and left-brain people. Usually this refers to a tendency to be either more nonverbal and intuitive, or more verbal and logical. In fact, some partners have a stronger right brain and weaker left brain. These partners tend to communicate and process threat with less emphasis on talk and more emphasis on feeling and expression. Other partners have a stronger left brain and a weaker right brain; their emphasis is more likely on logic, ideas, and talk, and less on feeling and emotional sensitivity. Of course, others are blessed with strong ambassadors of both types.

## STANDING IN EACH OTHER'S SHOES: THE ORBITOFRONTAL CORTEX

For a couple bubble to be created, all the ambassadors must work together in an atmosphere of friendliness, openness, kindness, lovingness, and other positive 'nesses. When they do so, it is under the direction of the *orbitofrontal cortex.* As ambassadors go, no other is as powerful and influential. Connected with almost every part of our brain, the orbitofrontal cortex is responsible for setting the stage for love. It is because of the orbitofrontal cortex that we are able to be curious about our mind and the minds of others. The orbitofrontal cortex is our moral and empathic center, and most importantly, can communicate with ambassadors and primitives alike. At times of impending war, it falls primarily to the orbitofrontal cortex to talk our primitives down. And the orbitofrontal cortex does this not so much by presenting a logical, debate-winning argument, as by providing feedback that enables the primitives to chill. It also allows us to feel empathy.

Neither Leia nor Franklin was able to step into the other's shoes, or simultaneously value and reckon with both points of view. Leia, for example, was so wrapped up in her own needs and desires that she didn't stop to consider the stresses and fears Franklin might be feeling. It didn't occur to her to ask what he was feeling, or to show appreciation for the fact that he might also be upset, for his own reasons. She simply expected him to conform to her views of the situation.

This basic inability to empathize may point to a poorly developed orbitofrontal cortex. Leia's orbitofrontal cortex could have been temporarily offline due to threat, and therefore unable to appreciate anything beyond her own ideas and feelings. Or it could have been disabled due to drug abuse or other medical reasons. Or perhaps, due to experiences during childhood, it never fully developed, making it difficult for her to empathize with and understand a partner's views and perspectives. In that case, even if she had another partner who was less reactive than Franklin, her orbitofrontal cortex would be no better equipped.

As long as Leia and Franklin—one or both—are unable to see, understand, and appreciate their partner's concerns or viewpoint, they will not be able to create a couple bubble. It will be difficult if not impossible for them to keep their love alive. However, if Leia's and Franklin's orbitofrontal cortices can operate properly, they will rein in their amygdalas and hypothalami at critical moments. Their smart vagi will remain engaged, and their right and left brains will act out of friendliness.

One solution to the problem of an offline orbitofrontal cortex is for partners to wait until they have calmed down enough to be able to make even the slightest gesture to help one another. Learning to remember to summon the help of the smart vagus and take a few deep breaths can help. Then, for instance, with even a modicum of calm, Franklin could have led with a sign of friendliness by saying something like "Honey, I love you and I understand where you're coming from. You're worried I'll never ask you to marry me. I understand, and I don't blame you for worrying." Such an act of friendliness and love disarms the primitives enough to enable the ambassadors to begin to come back online. As soon as Franklin senses their return, he can follow up with an appeal to Leia's ambassadors.

Most if not all of the recommendations in this book rest on the principle that you, as partners, need one another to keep love and avoid war. Initially, it can take time and some false starts. But eventually both of you must learn how to do this in a snap, without too much thought or talk. And that's easier, as we will see in the next chapter, if you have an owner's manual that includes instructions on what to do, and when, with your partner.

---

# EXERCISE: PRIMITIVES, MEET YOUR AMBASSADORS

You can practice this exercise with your partner.

Allow your primitives and ambassadors to hold a dialogue. Do this in the spirit of a parlor game, rather than as a means to solve a pressing relationship problem. The point is to become better acquainted with your primitives and ambassadors, to learn to recognize their respective voices. Of course, if important issues come up in the process, that's fine too.

Try any or all of the following combinations:

1. Have your primitives talk to your partner's primitives.

2. Have your primitives talk to your partner's ambassadors.

3. Have your ambassadors talk to your partner's primitives.

4. Have your ambassadors talk to your partner's ambassadors.

You might also try having your right brain interact with your partner's right brain. Then have your left brain interact with your partner's left brain. And then switch it up.

Examples of situations you might use include selecting from a menu at a restaurant (table 2.3), taking the dog for a walk, hanging a picture in the living room.

## TABLE 2.3   SAMPLE DIALOGUES: WHAT'S ON THE MENU?

| |
|---|
| *Primitives with Primitives* |
| You: (bordering on a whine) There's nothing here for me! <br> Partner: I'm getting steak. Why do you always have to be so fussy? <br> You: What? Now you want me to break my diet? <br> Partner: Did I say that? What's wrong with one of their salads? Put on your glasses and at least read the menu. |
| *Ambassadors with Ambassadors* |
| You: It looks like I might have to go with one of the salads if I want to stay on my diet. <br> Partner: Are you okay with that? Maybe we should go somewhere else. <br> You: Thanks for offering. But no, I'm just drooling 'cause there's so much here I can't have. <br> Partner: That's a bummer. I hope I don't make you drool more if I order the steak. |

What differences do you notice between the various interactions? As you become more familiar with the voices of your own and your partner's primitives and ambassadors, you can try this exercise with more significant topics.

# SECOND GUIDING PRINCIPLE

The second principle of this book is that *partners can make love and avoid war when their primitives are put at ease.* In this chapter, we have taken a journey through the brain, so to speak, to familiarize you with those aspects that are wired for war and those wired for love. Getting a sense of how these aspects work in your relationship is the first step in keeping love alive.

In the meantime, here are some supporting principles to guide you:

1. Identifying your primitives in action helps to hold them in check. Now that you know who your primitives are and how they operate, see if you can catch them in the act. When a red alert is going off, for example, can you recognize it for what it is? I'm not suggesting you will automatically know how to instantly turn it off. First simply recognize that your amygdalae are sounding an alarm. This alarm may take the form of your heart racing, palms sweating, face burning, or muscles tightening, or you may notice yourself suddenly becoming weak, slouched, nauseous, faint, numb, or shut down. In later chapters, I will discuss more specific techniques you and your partner can use when your primitives are running the show.

   Of course, identifying your primitives can be accomplished only by none other than...your ambassadors; specifically, your hippocampus. By definition, if you are able to notice your primitives in action, they can't have gained the upper hand. If they have, it's too late; better luck next time. And you can be assured that there most likely will be a next time.

2. It's always helpful to recognize what works well, in addition to what does not. For this reason, I also recommend identifying your ambassadors. Notice when they step up to the plate in support of your relationship; give them credit where credit is due. And invite them to step forward whenever their warmth, wisdom, and calm are needed.

   If your primitives are allowed to have their way—as sometimes happens—there will be no lollygagging around when danger's afoot. Life will be filled with one crisis after another, as you continually fire blind without thinking of the consequences. But when relationships are at stake, you want to avoid pulling the trigger. So call on your ambassadors to slow things down.

3. Identify your partner's primitives and ambassadors in action. At times, especially if your partner's primitives are large and in charge, you may

be able to do this before your partner can. Likewise, your partner sometimes may be able to do it for you before you can yourself. Find nonthreatening ways to let each other know what you have noticed. If possible, do this as close in time as you can to the actual incident.

Learning to recognize your partner's primitives and ambassadors gives you both a tool with which to better understand one another. This understanding is one important ingredient of a couple bubble. In the next chapter, we'll look more closely at what it means to really know your partner.

# CHAPTER 3

# Know Your Partner: How Does He or She Really Work?

W ho are we as relationship partners? How do we move toward and away from (both literally and figuratively) those upon whom we depend? It always amazes me that couples can be together for fifteen, twenty, even thirty years and the partners still feel they don't know each other. In so many ways, they don't know what makes each other tick.

As we saw in chapter 2, becoming acquainted with our primitives and ambassadors helps us answer these questions to some extent. But not everyone responds the same way in a relationship. The balance of power within and between the primitive and ambassador camps differs from person to person. Not everyone's ambassadors, for example, can rein in their primitives equally fast. In fact, due to the variance in your brains, you and your partner may experience different interactions between your primitives and ambassadors.

So, we each come to the table oriented toward a certain style of relating. We may recognize our partner's style, but often it is not on a conscious level. Unhappy partners often claim ignorance ("If I knew you were like this, I'd never have married you") and maintain claims of ignorance ("I just don't know what planet you're on") throughout the relationship. In this chapter, we explore why this mystification can occur, and what you can do to overcome it in your relationship.

As a couple therapist, I have come to know that such claims of ignorance are essentially untrue, even though they may feel true to the people who say them. They are untrue because we all have a style of relating that remains quite stable over time. Growing up, our parents' or caregivers' styles of relating set the standard by which we learned to adapt. Simply put, as we saw in chapter 2, our social wiring is set at an early age. Despite our intelligence and exposure to new ideas, this wiring remains virtually unchanged as we age. For instance, I commonly hear new parents say, "I will never do what my parents did to me," and yet despite their most ardent wishes not to repeat their parents' mistakes, in periods of distress they do exactly that. I don't say this with judgment; it's just a matter of human nature and biology.

Most partners audition for relationships fully unaware of who they are and how they are wired to relate in a committed couple universe. As in all auditions, they endeavor to put themselves forward in the best light. It wouldn't make sense for someone on the first date to say, "I spent a lot of time alone as a kid and I still do. I don't like my alone time to be intruded upon. I'll come to you when I'm ready. And don't bother coming to me, because then I'll think you're demanding something of me, and I don't like that." An equally quick way to send a date running for the hills would be to say, "I tend to be clingy, and to get angry when I feel abandoned. I hate silences and being ignored. I never seem to get enough from people, yet I don't take compliments well because I don't believe people are being sincere, so I tend to reject anything nice." During the initial phase of a relationship, partners may give clues about their basic predilections with regard to physical proximity, emotional intimacy, and concerns regarding safety and security. But it is only when the relationship becomes permanent in either or both partners' mind that these predilections really come to life.

Much of what we do, we do automatically and without thinking. This is largely the work of our primitives. In relationships, one of the things partners typically are unaware of is how they physically move toward and away from each other. Our brain's reaction to physical proximity and duration of proximity is wired from early childhood, and influences such things as where we choose to stand or sit in relation to one another, how we adjust distance between us, how we embrace, how we make love, and just about everything we do that involves physical movement and static physical space. Because we operate largely on automatic pilot, we remain oblivious to this entire dimension of our interactions. Moreover, we handle physical proximity differently during courtship than in more committed phases of relationship. For example, many couples touch constantly while they're dating, but the frequency with which they touch drops off dramatically after they make a commitment. This can be very confusing, and can lead partners to wonder, "Do I even know who you are anymore?"

# "WHO ARE YOU?"

No one likes to be classified, yet we tend to classify the people and things around us because we have brains that, by nature, organize, sort, and compare information and experience. In fact, people have been defining the human condition for centuries, and they continue to form new ways of doing so today. We are liberals or conservatives, geeks or Goths, atheists or religious fanatics, Scorpios or Capricorns, either from Mars or from Venus. As long as we don't use these categories to debase or dehumanize anyone, they can help us understand one another.

A key premise of this book is that partners can benefit from having an owner's manual for one another and for their relationship. An important function of this manual is that it allows you to define, describe, and ultimately label your partner's predilections and relationship style. If you can recognize and understand each other's styles, it is much easier to work together and to resolve issues as they arise. Having the sense that "I know who you are" makes it easier to be forgiving and to be sincerely supportive.

The styles I present here are neither new nor entirely my own. They are drawn from research findings, first made popular by John Bowlby (1969) and Mary Ainsworth and her colleagues (Ainsworth, Bell, and Stayton 1971) almost half a century ago, explaining how infants form attachments. Over the years, I have observed that most partners fall into one of three main relationship styles. I offer these styles to you with a couple of caveats.

First, if you find you can't decide which style best fits your partner or yourself, don't try to force it. I have presented the styles in their pure form; in reality, the "mileage you get" from this information may vary. Although the vast majority of people do identify with one or another of these three styles, not everyone does. In fact, people can be a blend of different styles, which sometimes makes it difficult to pick the most salient one. If this is the case for you, no worries. You can keep both in mind and use whichever fits best in a given situation.

Second, my purpose in describing these styles is to inspire respect and understanding for what I believe to be normal human traits. Please do not take them as character defects. Definitely don't turn them into ammunition against your partner. Rather, see these styles as representing the natural and necessary adaptations each of us makes as we develop into adulthood.

# HOW WE DEVELOP OUR STYLE OF RELATING

As I've stated, our social wiring is set at an early age. Whether we grow up feeling basically secure or basically insecure is determined by how our parents or caregivers relate to us and to the world. Parents who put a high value on relationship tend to do more to protect their loved ones than do parents who value other things more. They tend to spend more face-to-face and skin-to-skin time with their child; be more curious about and interested in their child's mind; be more focused, attentive, and attuned to their child's needs; and generally be more motivated to quickly correct errors or injuries, because they want to restore the goodness of the relationship. In these ways, they create a secure environment for the child.

The dynamics of this early relationship leave their mark at a physiological level. Neuroscientists have observed that children who receive lots of positive attention from adults tend to develop more neural networks than do children deprived of social interaction with adult brains. The primitives and ambassadors of secure children tend to be well integrated, and so these children generally are able to handle their emotions and impulses. Their amygdalae aren't overcharged and their hypothalamus conducts normal operations and feedback communication with the pituitary and adrenal glands, the other cogs in the threat and stress wheel, turning that system on and off when appropriate. Their dumb vagus and smart vagus are well balanced.

Because of good relationships early in life, secure children tend to have a well-developed right brain and insula, so they are adept at reading faces, voices, emotions, and body sensations, and at getting the overall gist of things.

In particular, their orbitofrontal cortex is well developed, with neural connections that provide feedback to their other ambassadors and their primitives. Compared with insecure children, they tend to have more empathy, better moral judgment, greater control over impulses, and more consistent management of frustration. In general, secure children are more resilient to the slings and arrows of social-emotional stress and do far better in social situations.

A secure relationship is characterized by playfulness, interaction, flexibility, and sensitivity. Good feelings predominate because any bad feelings are quickly soothed. It's a great place to be! It's a place where we can expect fun and excitement and novelty, but also relief and comfort and shelter. When we experience this kind of secure foundation as a child, we carry it forth into adulthood. We become what I'm calling an anchor.

However, not all of us had relationships in early childhood that felt secure. Perhaps we had several rotating caregivers, without one who was consistently available or dependable. Or perhaps we had one or more caregivers who primarily valued something else more than relationship, such as self-preservation, beauty, youth, performance, intelligence, talent, money, or reputation. Maybe one or more caregivers emphasized loyalty, privacy, independence, and self-sufficiency over relationship fidelity. Almost anything can supplant the value of relationship, and often when this occurs, it is not by choice. A caregiver's mental or physical illness, unresolved trauma or loss, immaturity, and the like can interfere with a child's sense of security. If this happens to us, then as adults we come to relationships with an underlying insecurity. That can lead us to keep to ourselves and avoid too much contact, instead viewing ourselves as an island in the ocean of humanity. Or it can lead to ambivalence about connecting with others, in which case we become more like a wave.

# EXERCISE: TAKE A SNAPSHOT OF YOUR CHILDHOOD

As you wonder about your own childhood, you might ask yourself if any of the following happened when you were a child:

♥ Was I frequently left alone to play by myself?

- ♥ Was I taken out as a show item and then put away when no longer needed?

- ♥ Was I expected to meet the needs of my caregivers more than my own needs?

- ♥ Was I expected to manage my caregivers' emotional world or self-esteem?

- ♥ Was I expected to stay young, cute, and dependent?

- ♥ Was I expected to grow up quickly, act self-sufficient, and not be a problem?

- ♥ Were my caregivers sensitive to my needs or did they frequently misread me?

Before we go further, I want to clarify that this snapshot of your childhood is not about whether or not you were loved by your parents. I don't want to give the impression I'm talking about *love*. What I'm describing has less to do with love and more to do with safety and security and the underlying attitudes we bring to a relationship.

## THREE STYLES OF RELATING

When speaking about attachment styles, psychologists use terms such as *securely attached, insecurely avoidant,* and *insecurely ambivalent.* To keep it a bit lighter here, I'm going to substitute the terms *anchor, island,* and *wave.*

Clearly there are advantages to being an anchor. Given the option, most of us would choose to feel secure over not. But we all bring something different to the table. Imagine what a boring place this world would be if it were any other way. To help you keep this in focus, I'd like to begin by summarizing the strengths of each type, in table 3.1.

TABLE 3.1  STRENGTHS OF THE
THREE STYLES OF RELATING

| Style | Strengths of people who relate in this style |
|---|---|
| Anchor | Secure as individuals<br><br>Willing to commit and fully share with another<br><br>Generally happy people<br><br>Adapt easily to the needs of the moment |
| Island | Independent and self-reliant<br><br>Take good care of themselves<br><br>Productive and creative, especially when given space<br><br>Low maintenance |
| Wave | Generous and giving<br><br>Focused on taking care of others<br><br>Happiest when around other people<br><br>Able to see both sides of an issue |

As you read about the three couples in this chapter and learn more about the three styles, see which style best reflects the relationship styles of yourself and your partner.

# THE ANCHOR: "TWO CAN BE BETTER THAN ONE."

Mary and Pierce have been together for twenty-five years. They raised two children, both now out of the home. These days, Mary and Pierce spend more time dealing with their aging parents than with issues related to their own offspring. When Pierce's widowed mother was diagnosed with Alzheimer's disease, the couple found themselves struggling with the various options. Both have rewarding but demanding careers in the legal field, and as much as they would have liked to bring Pierce's mother into their home for care, they had to acknowledge that would not be realistic.

Their conversations during the process of arriving at the decision to find a medical facility for Pierce's mother went something like this.

"I want you to tell me exactly how you feel," Mary says, looking intently at Pierce so as not to miss any subtle communication written on his face.

"Of course, you know I always do," says Pierce. "Honestly, since we had that long talk the other night, I have to say I'm feeling a degree of relief."

"You mean since we discussed moving your mom out of her home?"

"Right." He pauses, looking deeply into Mary's eyes, not hiding the pain still hovering beneath his relief. "I think it's taken a load off me to realize that staying here might not be the best life for her."

"You know, I was worried you might be upset with me when I first said what I thought would be best," Mary says quickly. "I wasn't sure we were on the same page. My parents are still healthy, so this isn't the same experience for me."

Pierce smiles. "Yes, I admit I was pretty upset at first. But I thought about it. I knew you were trying to figure out what would be best for all of us—you, me, and my mother."

"Exactly," says Mary. "If it were my mom, I'd want the same from you. This isn't about getting my way. It's about us, together. If you strongly believe we should find a way to bring your mom here, at least for a while, I'll work with you on that. I might disagree. But I certainly won't fight you."

"Thanks," says Pierce. "And thanks for not overreacting when I started to get kind of uptight."

"Honey, I had a pretty good sense of what was happening for you," Mary says gently, then pauses and continues with a twinkle in her eye. "You know, after all these years, I have the manual on you."

Pierce smiles back. "You sure do, and I'm so glad—even if it's a heck of a long manual, with all my quirks and foibles."

Mary gives a little chuckle. "You know I wouldn't have you any other way. Besides, the manual you have on me isn't exactly the abridged version."

Pierce pauses and sighs deeply. "When I think about it rationally, it's obvious that it wouldn't work to bring mom here."

"Honey, if we put our heads together, we can find ways to make the best of the situation. For example, getting your mom a place that's close by. And arranging our schedules so we can both visit her as much as possible…" Mary stops because she sees Pierce nodding his head and his eyes tearing up.

"And bring her here for meals as often as we can," he says, picking up where Mary left off. She wipes a teardrop off his cheek, and he grabs her hand and kisses it. "Actually, I think I'll feel better once I see my mom well taken care of in a good environment."

"I know you will," says Mary, "And we'll keep talking. Whatever comes up, we'll deal with it. As we always do, yeah?"

"Yup. You know," Pierce adds, giving her a hug, "I so appreciate being able to talk with you about all this. We make a good team."

## WE CAN DO IT TOGETHER

Mary and Pierce are examples of two anchors. They each came to the relationship feeling secure in themselves as individuals. Of course, anchors don't always choose to be with other anchors. An anchor can mate with an island or a wave. In many cases, these matches result in the other partner becoming more of an anchor. Let me say this again because it is important: anchors can pull non-anchors into becoming anchors themselves. Of course, the reverse can occur, as well. An island or wave can pull an anchor into becoming more insecure.

As anchors, Mary and Pierce are able to offer this security to one another because they experienced and learned from early caregivers who placed a high value on relationship and interaction. Their parents were attuned, responsive, and sensitive to their signals of distress, bids for comfort, and efforts to communicate. Both Mary and Pierce have memories of being held, hugged, kissed, and rocked as a child. They recall seeing a loving gleam in their parents' eyes that they knew was meant just for them.

Neither Mary nor Pierce feels the other is overly needy or clings to him or her. And neither feels anxious about getting too close or moving too far away. When they have to be apart for some reason, they make frequent contact by phone and e-mail, greeting each other with liveliness and good cheer. Together or apart, they are unafraid to fully share one another's minds without concern about any negative consequences, as was the case when Mary made known what she thought would be best for Pierce's mom. They respect each other's feelings and treat one another as the first source to share good news and bad news. Each takes careful notice of the other in private and in public, minding cues that signal distress and responding quickly to provide relief. In all these ways, they build a mutual appreciation for their couple bubble and regard themselves as stewards of their mutual sense of safety and security. Each has made the effort to learn how the other works and to compile what amounts to a manual with all this knowledge, and they make use of it on a daily, if not moment-to-moment, basis.

This couple truly view themselves to be in each other's care, and understand that the lifeline they maintain, their tether to each other, is what gives them the energy and courage needed to face the daily stresses and challenges of the real world. Because their relationship is secure, they are able to continually turn to it and use it as their anchoring device amidst the sometimes chaotic outer world.

Anchors aren't perfect people, but they are generally happy people. They are given to feelings of gratefulness for the things and people in their lives. People tend to be drawn to anchors because of their strength of character, love of people, and complexity. They adapt easily to the needs of the moment. They can make decisions and bear the consequences.

Anchors take good care of themselves and their relationships. They expect committed partnerships to be mutually satisfying, supportive, and respectful, and will not bother with unsafe or nonreciprocal relationships. They do not give up on a relationship if the going gets rough, or when they become frustrated. They are unafraid to admit errors and are quick to mend injuries or misunderstandings as they arise. They handle moments of togetherness with the same ease as they handle separation from their partner. In these ways, they are good at coping with relationship challenges that might overwhelm non-anchors.

## EXERCISE: ARE YOU AN ANCHOR?

Do you believe yourself or your partner might be an anchor? Look at this checklist and see if it fits—first for yourself, and then for your partner.

♥ "I'm fine by myself, but I prefer the give-and-take of an intimate relationship."

♥ "I value my close relationships and will do what it takes to keep them in good condition."

♥ "I get along with a wide variety of people."

♥ "I love people, and people tend to love me."

♥ "My close relationships aren't fragile."

♥ "Lots of physical contact and affection is fine with me."

♥ "I'm equally relaxed when I'm with my partner and when I'm alone."

♥ "Interruptions by my loved ones do not bother me."

Now let's look at a couple who operate under a very different style.

# The Island: "I Want You in the House, Just Not in My Room... Unless I Ask You."

Chiana and Carlos, both professionals in their early forties, decided early in their marriage not to have children and instead to embellish their relationship with plenty of travel and adventure. Chiana had held off on getting married because she felt her career as a journalist didn't allow her time to devote to another person. But then she met Carlos, and he seemed like a kindred spirit. After their wedding, they built a home that included two separate areas: his and hers. Carlos had his own music room, with a small bed for nights when he wished to stay up late. Chiana designed an office where she could write and watch television without being disturbed. Their master bedroom was wired with high-speed Internet so both could use it on respective sides of their oversized king.

Problems arose shortly after their wedding. Chiana's interest in sex started to wane. Carlos was accustomed to taking turns initiating sex, but Chiana stopped making moves and started rejecting his advances. The intense eye contact they had so often enjoyed during courtship was replaced by television shows, movies, and conversations from across the room. Although Carlos was the first to complain of loneliness, his behavior was not entirely dissimilar from hers.

Arguments about their lack of intimacy began to go like this:

"I still love you," Chiana explains, after they've come home from work and Carlos has made an advance she's rejected. "It's just we're so busy. Plus you know how I feel about staying in shape."

Carlos's face turns red. "So you're blaming me for not having sex? It's my fault because I haven't been working out? Is that what you're saying?"

"Don't put words in my mouth. I'm saying we're both busy."

"No, I distinctly heard you say you're not into sex because I'm out of shape. That's ridiculous! I'm in great shape, and you know it. If I told you something like that, you'd never talk to me again."

"Look," Chiana says impatiently, "let's talk later. I've got a deadline and can't deal with this right now." She picks up her laptop and heads briskly for her office down the hall.

Later that evening, Carlos puts finishing touches on the dinner he's cooked. He calls for Chiana, but there's no response. So he approaches her office and opens the door.

Chiana, her back turned, barks, "Not now!"

Knowing she hates to be disturbed, Carlos stays in the doorway. "Don't you want the dinner I made for us?"

There's a long silence, during which Carlos grows increasingly irritated. "Chiana!" he says sharply, trying to get her attention, but afraid of stepping any closer.

"What do you want?" she screams, turning and slapping her hands hard on her legs. "I told you, not now!" She pivots back to her computer.

Carlos sighs deeply. "So, when can I expect you?"

"I'll be there as soon as I can. Fifteen minutes, okay?

With that, Carlos leaves. But he's back twenty minutes later.

Chiana, still working fervently, senses his presence. "That wasn't fifteen minutes," she snaps.

"You're correct. It was twenty," Carlos says calmly.

"No it wasn't," she counters.

Deflated, Carlos again turns to leave. But his irritation is rising. "How much of this am I supposed to take?" he mutters.

Chiana slams a file onto her desk, turns around, and screams, "You say you want me to be successful, but you keep sabotaging me!"

After a brief stare-off, Carlos relents. "Fine! Make your own dinner. I'm out of here!" He leaves, slamming the door behind him.

## I CAN DO IT MYSELF

Now, before you jump to judge Chiana, let's get something straight: she's not doing anything outside of her nature. She is an island. Her main problem, if we want to call it that, is that she doesn't understand what her relationship style is. And perhaps more importantly in this instance, Carlos doesn't understand it, either. Both of them are islands, but for simplicity's sake, we're going to look closely only at Chiana.

Chiana is not purposely trying to ruin her marriage. Quite the contrary, she's doing what she knows best from her own experience. And so, by the way, is Carlos. First and foremost, we need to realize that Chiana's actions and reactions have a basis in her physical makeup. Her understanding about how to move toward and away from others, about how to signal others, and about the kind of response she anticipates getting from others is built into her nervous system. These patterns have been there from a very early age; she is merely following suit now.

Chiana's anger at her husband's intrusion is, in her mind, fully justified. In defense, she shrugs and says, "Wouldn't anybody in my position do the same?" Let's look at how Chiana's relationship history led her to became an island, and what this means for her relationship with Carlos.

Chiana was an only child who spent a good deal of time by herself. Both her parents were working professionals, and they employed a nanny to watch over their daughter. Chiana describes her mother as brilliant but not especially touchy-feely. Her parents sometimes read aloud to her, but she can't recall either coming to her when she cried or called out at night. Her inability to recall loving moments causes Chiana anxiety. She feels she is betraying her parents, who she strongly believes loved and cared for her. After all, they always gave her what she needed, she tells herself. She has happy family photos to prove it!

In fact, there is nothing wrong with Chiana's memory. She can recall, for example, feeling hurt as a teenager by her father's disapproval. She has a vivid memory of being afraid her mother was angry at her as they were leaving a toy store. These events did happen, and they were pivotal determinants of her current relationship style. Her lack of positive memories simply reflects the dearth of positive events in her early home life.

In a nutshell, we can say that the sum total of her experiences—the positive and the negative; those she can recall and those she cannot—shaped Chiana into an island. Because her mother rarely sought physical contact, Chiana learned it was better not to look to others for affection. Instead, she focused on taking care of herself. As a single adult, she had no difficulty interacting with other adults. People saw her as smart and creative, and she developed a wide circle of friends who shared her interests.

When Chiana married Carlos, however, he became the home she experienced in childhood. She does not expect frequent interactions with him, including sexual intimacy. Although she enjoys his company, she finds it hard to shift out of her alone time. His bids for attention often feel jarring, as if he were trying to make her do something against her will. She tends to resist until he has coaxed her to come closer and engage with him. Once this shift is made, she adjusts and enjoys being with him. However, when left alone for even a few minutes, she again becomes absorbed in her private world.

As an island, Chiana believes her alone time is a choice and a preference. She is unaware it's a consequence of her need to depend and connect having been met with unresponsiveness, dismissiveness, and insensitivity when she was an infant. People who are islands often confuse independence and autonomy with their adaptation to neglect. As we saw in chapter 1, in order to achieve true autonomy, it is necessary to first experience being loved by and taken care of by another person.

I want to reiterate: there is nothing inherently wrong with being an island. Merely conjuring up the image of lounging on a lush tropical island is enough for many people to feel a rush of endorphins. In the context of a couple's relationship, however, difficulties can arise if one or both partners are addicted to alone time, especially if they don't know it. Instead of seeking the closeness of a couple bubble, the addicted partner avoids it. Feelings of loneliness are obscured by the dreamlike state generated during alone time.

Islands tend to experience more interpersonal stress than do waves or anchors. This is due to their higher sense of threat in the presence of their significant others, as well as in social situations in general. Whereas waves or anchors may feel shy, islands can be overly sensitive to perceived intrusions by a partner. Especially if their partner is not another island, islands may fear their need for distance may result in disaster. Two islands can court disaster simply through their high tolerance for being apart from one another. For example, when Carlos is away on business, Chiana doesn't feel a loss. Her relief at the absence of interpersonal stress is greater than her awareness of loss or of being left. If tolerating time alone were comparable to holding one's breath underwater, islands could hold their breath much longer than anybody else.

Islands tend to look toward the future and avoid looking at present relationship conflicts or past relationships, including those in childhood. Their mantra is "That's the past," with the implication that rehashing history would be pointless. In point of fact, islands often idealize or demonize their past and are unable to call up specifics. Common refrains when asked about details include "I don't remember," "It doesn't matter," "Who cares?" and so on. This tendency can become extremely frustrating for the other partner.

Without the help of their partner, islands are unlikely to understand who they are, recognize their deep-seated existential loneliness, or ultimately overcome their anxiety about intimate relationship. After all, they know only what they've experienced. In order to step off their islands and into a more social world, they need to be met with understanding. They need partners who will make the effort to find out what makes them tick. This isn't to say it's impossible for two islands to, for example, create a couple bubble. But without some form of help, the odds are against it.

---

# EXERCISE: ARE YOU AN ISLAND?

Do you recognize yourself and/or your partner from our discussion thus far? Here are some statements that are typical of an island. See if any ring a bell for you—either for yourself or your partner.

♥ "I know how to take care of myself better than anyone else could."

♥ "I'm a do-it-myself kind of person."

♥ "I thrive when I can spend time in my own private sanctuary."

♥ "If you upset me, I have to be by myself to calm down."

♥ "I often feel my partner wants or needs something from me that I can't give."

♥ "I'm most relaxed when nobody else is around."

♥ "I'm low maintenance, and I prefer a partner who also is low maintenance."

# THE WAVE: "IF ONLY YOU LOVED ME LIKE I LOVE YOU."

Now let's meet another couple. Married for seventeen years, Jaden and Kaylee had two small children and lived in a modest two-bedroom house in the suburbs. Kaylee was a stay-at-home mom, and Jaden worked a nine-to-five job.

When they finally sought therapy for their problems, Kaylee complained that Jaden was often angry about everything: "He's angry with me, he's angry with the kids, he's angry with his boss . . . it's like nothing we do is enough, and I'm getting sick and tired of having to deal with his temper tantrums."

Jaden thought Kaylee was not acknowledging his reasons for feeling angry and upset. Unable to sit quietly and listen to her even for a few moments at a time, he expressed himself with grunts and groans and facial expressions of shock and surprise.

Their dialogue in couples therapy would go like this:

"I look forward to seeing you all day, but I don't think you even miss me at all. I call or text message, and you don't respond. It's like I'm bugging you or something. Do you know how many wives would give their right arm for a husband who misses them during the day, who really wants to connect?" Jaden says with a perplexed look on his face.

"But you call me all the time!" Kaylee responds, eyes widened in a gesture that suggests he's clueless. "I don't get a chance to miss you. And if you miss me so much, why do you come home so pissed off and surly?"

"I . . . I don't . . . You think I'm surly?" He laughs. "I don't think I'm surly."

Kaylee looks at him as if expecting him to think about it.

"You're right," he admits after a minute. "I do get angry when I see the kids out of control and the house in disarray. I'm exhausted from work, and it feels like you're just ignoring me."

"That's not true," Kaylee interrupts. "Often I come to you, and you just yell at me. If I say something nice, you say something mean in return."

"I don't say anything mean," he retorts, defending himself. "I'm not a mean person. You must be talking about yourself. You can be cold, and you've admitted it. I'm the opposite of cold. When I call you during the day or ask to spend time with you at night, you're always busy, like you don't have time for me. And you never say anything nice to me."

Kaylee, looking exasperated, takes a deep breath and says, "You just don't remember the nice things I say. Or you throw them back in my face and say I don't mean it. Really, Jaden, it makes me not want to be near you. And it's not just me; if either of the boys fails to pay attention to you, you become furious and take it personally."

Jaden responds by throwing his legs out in front of him and tossing his arms above his head, with his eyes facing the heavens. "I really feel misunderstood. I'm not the bad guy. Do you know that every time there's a special occasion, like our anniversary, I have to plan it? Do you think you could ever take the initiative? You don't remember Father's Day," he starts counting on his fingers, "you don't know what to get me for my birthday.... Let's see, you don't even want to have sex with me, for goodness sake!"

Kaylee looks down at the floor and says, "You're impossible."

"I know. You've always felt I'm impossible, I'm just way too much trouble. Why don't you leave me, if you feel that way? You're sorry you married me, aren't you?"

Kaylee continues to look down, but now with her arms folded and her head shaking.

# I CAN'T DO IT WITH OR WITHOUT YOU.

Now, before you get angry at Jaden, remember he's not really doing anything wrong. As with Chiana, his reaction to his partner is quite reasonable when you consider that it's based on his experience not just with her, but with his earliest caregivers. In fact, both Chiana's and Jaden's insecurity preceded their current relationships. In other words, they both came to the table this way, even if they don't realize it.

Jaden responds as he does because he is a wave. Ocean waves don't provide any sense of steadiness or security. They cause a perpetual disturbance of the water—always going up and down, up and down. From the vantage point of the shore, waves come rushing in, only to immediately rush back out again. It's as if they can't make up their mind where they belong. In the case of partners, it's the wave who causes disturbance in the relationship by becoming preoccupied with fear, anger, and ambivalence about being close. They can't fully move forward because they are still caught up with past injuries and injustices. These thoughts and emotions ebb and flow like literal waves.

If both members of the couple are waves, there can be even more turmoil—a continual tug of war, as both partners alternate between being close and being standoffish. So, if you are a wave, or in a relationship with one, prepare for a certain amount of high drama. Unlike islands, who are likely to do a disappearing act when the going gets tough, waves respond by, well . . . making waves.

Jaden's ambivalence stems from the fact that he both wants to connect and is afraid of connecting. He alternates between feeling wanted and rejected. He thinks it's only a matter of time before Kaylee will reject him, so he holds back from feeling good, hopeful, relieved, and comforted. As Jaden puts it, "Better to reject before being rejected, better to leave before being left." He comes in close to his partner, hoping for connection, then quickly pulls back, anticipating disappointment. This moving in, then pulling back is the sign of a wave. The fact that Kaylee is an island—did you notice?—and therefore naturally pulls away in times of stress only serves to accentuate Jaden's tendencies.

Unlike Chiana, Jaden remembers his childhood very well and remains angry at his parents, as if time has stood still. While Chiana idealizes her past and is unaware of having been on the receiving end of any injustice, Jaden is supremely aware of having been the victim of selfishness and insensitivity. He feels ripped off, both then and now. Unlike Chiana, he received plenty of affection, particularly from his mother, who often kissed, held, and rocked him. But he tends to focus on the times she was frustrated with him. Then, she was too anxious to deal with his fears, and too preoccupied with her own life to deal with his needs. Jaden's father frequently was unavailable, which led to fights between his parents. Once, when his father left the house and stayed at a hotel, his mother cried and asked Jaden to stay with her through the night. He was only seven years old.

In contrast with Chiana, Jaden always valued interacting with others, especially his parents. He liked spending time talking, playing games, and cuddling. He loved to talk so much he often felt he was being "a pain in the ass." It's not as if he made this up. Both parents implied as much to him. What Jaden remembers disliking most intensely was being left or ignored. His parents sometimes left him with a babysitter, causing him great distress. He hated sleepovers that took him away from home and his parents.

Jaden truly does not understand why he reacts with anger whenever he reunites with Kaylee after they've been apart. His reaction confuses him as much as it bothers her.

"I really miss her and think about her when we're apart," he says. "I imagine us cuddling and having a great evening together. But then I come home, and something comes over me. I feel instantly angry, like I'm drowning but I don't know why. She'll say something like, 'I'm glad you're home,' and I'll believe her. And yet I'll say something like, 'You're just glad 'cause you need me to fix the leaky faucet.' It's not like I intend to insult her, but I'm worried about what she's really feeling. She finds me annoying. And I am, you know. I really am a pain in the ass," he says, eyes filling with tears.

Whereas Chiana denies her need to depend on someone and would feel ashamed if she realized how needy she is, Jaden is aware of his need to depend. However, he believes he is too much for anyone, and anticipates being dropped, abandoned, or punished. This anticipation is so strong that he creates that reaction in his partner through his anger and negativity. He pushes on her until she pushes back.

Chiana refuses to look back and avoids dealing with current conflicts. Jaden refuses to look forward, and therefore is stuck focusing on the past and remains preoccupied with current conflicts. He won't move forward because he feels he hasn't resolved current and past injustices and insensitivities, nor received assurance that rejection or abandonment will never again occur.

Jaden's insecurity can appear bottomless, and his need for frequent contact and reassurance can appear unreasonable to his partner. But neither of these is really true. Jaden's issues probably are being maintained because both he and Kaylee have a misperception about relationships. They have not created a couple bubble, and they don't have an agreement to put their relationship first. If Kaylee overcame her island tendencies and cheerfully made herself available to Jaden during the day, understanding that contact with him served her, as well, Jaden's need to check and recheck her availability would subside. If Jaden cheerfully respected Kaylee's need to get off the phone quickly, her anxiety about feeling "trapped" or "set up" would diminish. This mutual sensitivity would ease Jaden's perception that their time apart was a precursor to abandonment, and alleviate Kaylee's perception that she must constantly babysit Jaden so he feels secure.

To bring healing to their relationship, Kaylee would have to experiment with something counterintuitive. Instead of pulling away, she would have to move physically and emotionally forward and douse Jaden with messages such as "I'm so glad to see you" or "I missed you so much" or "Come here, you grouch, and give your girl a big kiss." Of course, this is easier said than done, and most partners like Kaylee would balk at such a suggestion. Nonetheless, if your partner is a wave, this is the best way to overcome childhood injuries and shift him or her quickly from feeling threatened to feeling loved. When this happens, you benefit, as well.

Jaden also must do something different. He must come back to Kaylee as soon as he realizes he's been negative or hostile, and apologize.

In these ways, they can repair the breach in their relationship and stop pushing each other away.

---

# EXERCISE: ARE YOU A WAVE?

Do you think you and/or your partner might be a wave? Here are some typical statements; see if they apply to your or to your partner:

♥   "I take better care of others than I do of myself."

♥ "I often feel as though I'm giving and giving, and not getting anything back."

♥ "I thrive on talking to and interacting with others."

♥ "If you upset me, I have to talk in order to calm down."

♥ "My partner tends to be rather selfish and self-centered."

♥ "I'm most relaxed when I'm around my friends."

♥ "Love relationships are ultimately disappointing and exhausting. You can never really depend on anyone."

# Ambassadors Gone Wild

Whatever your style—anchor, island, or wave—you and your partner may assume, from what you've read so far, that you can count on your ambassadors to maintain harmony between you. For the most part, this is a good assumption. However, as I mentioned in chapter 2, despite their good qualities and benevolent intentions, ambassadors can be quite obnoxious at times. It's true: the ambassadors can go wild—or wimpy or just plain weird—in all of us, no exceptions.

Anchors tend to have the most balanced ambassadors. On the rare occasion that some of their ambassadors go wild, anchors possess other ambassadors that can corral the wayward ones pretty quickly. Islands and waves, on the other hand, often grapple with more serious ambassador disparities. During times of distress, islands and waves have one thing in common: both have an ineffectual orbitofrontal cortex. The orbitofrontal cortex, you will recall, is the ruler of ambassadors and primitives alike. It's our orbitofrontal cortex, ultimately, that determines whether or not we go to war. For this reason, islands and waves are more at risk of going to war if their ambassadors get wild or otherwise fail to toe the line.

## THE WILD ISLAND

Islands tend to have both heightened primitives and wild ambassadors. If your partner is an island, he or she may rely too much on talking to work out issues. This often is a consequence of not being able to connect readily on a nonverbal level. Of course, this imbalance is natural for an island and generally may not lead to complaints in settings other than romantic relationships. When the relationship becomes distressed, a left brain gone wild can get your partner into hot water if he or she comes across as overly logical, rational, arrogant, unemotional, or unexpressive, or as insufficiently empathic. Under stress, an island can be overly terse, dismissive, and inflexible, or too silent or too still.

During conflict, an island will tend focus on the future and avoid the present and past. "The past is past. Why can't we just move forward?" is a common island approach. In all-out war, an island's left brain gets hijacked by primitives and can become threatening by communicating attack or retreat. Rendered useless to social or creative causes, it uses words (or the withholding of words) as weapons. It still sounds like an ambassador, but it acts like a primitive: its only interest is survival.

Two left brains at war can get ugly. To avoid this, ideally you can ride to the rescue and get through with verbal friendliness. Provided your own left brain has not gone wild, talk your partner down. Be reassuring, calming, and rational ("I understand what you're saying and it makes sense" or "You're right about that" or "You make a good point").

A wild island often has little sense of what he or she is feeling and is poor at communicating feelings or picking up the feelings of his or her partner. The partner of an island may also have trouble doing these things, regardless of whether that person is an island too.

## THE WILD WAVE

If your partner is a wave, he or she may insist too much on verbal assurances of love and security. This is the reverse of what we see with an island, who is less prone to seek or even care about such assurances. With a right brain gone wild, your partner may appear overly preoccupied with these assurances, and appear overly expressive, dramatic, emotional, tangential, irrational, and angry. Under stress, a wave can be unforgiving, punishing, rejecting, and inflexible.

During conflict, a wave will tend to focus on the past and avoid the present and future. "I can't move forward until we resolve what happened" is a common wave statement. In all-out war, the wave's right brain gets hijacked by primitives and can become threatening by doggedly pursuing a resolution through connecting, now! In this situation, the connector uses physical and emotional connection as weapons. Again, it still sounds like an ambassador, but it acts like a primitive.

To avoid the explosiveness of two right brains at war, try reaching out nonverbally to your partner. If your own right brain has not gone wild, disarm your partner through nonverbal friendliness. Touch him or her gently; provide a calm presence. When you do speak, be reassuring and soothing.

# THIRD GUIDING PRINCIPLE

The third principle of this book is that *partners relate to one another primarily as anchors, islands, or waves*. You and your partner should become familiar with each others' relationship styles.

We get to know our partner fully in order to become competent as managers of our partners in the best way. By competent managers, I mean partners who are experts on one another and know how to move, shift, motivate, influence, soothe, and inspire one another. In contrast, partners who are not experts on one another tend to create a mutual sense of threat and insecurity. They don't enjoy a couple bubble. These partners also tend to wish the other would change, listen to them, or do things the way they do, and ultimately believe they coupled with the wrong person. Sadly, these partners merely recreate the insensitivity, injustice, and insecurity of their childhood, never really knowing what is within their reach "if only ...."

For many people, closeness brings both the promise of safety and security and a threat to safety and security. This raises the question, how do you get what you want and need from a relationship, while avoiding what you fear might happen? This quandary is similar to stealing honey without being stung by a bee. The degree to which we must work to get the honey, while avoiding getting stung, in intimate relationships is the degree to which we feel fundamentally insecure. But here's the rub: if we feel insecure about close relationships, there is no way to become more secure without being in one. No book or audiotape, workshop, or religion can alter our sense of relationship security. In other words, as far as relationships go, we are hurt by people and yet we can be healed only by people.

And that's good news. It is entirely possible to become an anchor by spending time in a close, dependent, secure relationship with another person. That person can be a therapist, or it can be a primary romantic partner who is an anchor or close to becoming one. Though the purpose of this book is not specifically to convert you or your partner into anchors, its principles will guide you toward a more secure relationship. Spend enough time in a secure relationship, and you'll become an anchor!

Here are some supporting principles to guide you:

1. Discover your partner. Using the examples presented in this chapter, find out what you may not yet know about your partner. What relationship style best describes your partner? And while you're at it, what style best describes you? As I mentioned before, please resist the temptation to use this typology as ammunition against one another. Like any powerful tool, it can inflict damage if used improperly. So use it with compassion in your relationship.

2. Be unapologetically you. Our task in committed relationships is not to change or become a different person. Quite the contrary: our task is to be unapologetically ourselves. Home is not a place to feel chronically ashamed or to pretend we are someone we're not. Rather, we can be ourselves while retaining our sense of responsibility to others and to ourselves. And just as we are unapologetically ourselves, we must encourage our partner to be unapologetically himself or herself. In this way, we offer each other unconditional acceptance.

   Of course, being unapologetically ourselves doesn't mean we are reckless or uncaring about how we treat others, or that we can use this as an excuse to be our worst selves. For example, if your partner is unfaithful or otherwise hurtful to you, he or she can't simply say, "Tough. This is who am. Just accept it." No. This is a time when apology is definitely in order. In fact, whenever your partner voices hurt, you need to focus less on being unapologetically yourself and more on tending to your partner's needs and concerns. Remember the first guiding principle: *creating a couple bubble allows partners to keep each other safe and secure.* Your mandate is to be unapologetically yourself as long as you also keep your partner safe.

3. Don't try to change your partner. You could say that we all change, and also that we never change. Both are true. And this is why acceptance is so important. We can and do change our attitudes, our behaviors, and even our brains over time. However, the fundamental wiring that takes place during our earliest experiences stays with us from cradle to grave. Of course, we can change this wiring in phenomenal ways through corrective relationships. Sometime these changes transform all but the last remnants of our remembered fears and injuries. But this should not be the goal of a couple's relationship. No one changes from fundamentally insecure to fundamentally secure under conditions of fear, duress, disapproval, or threat of abandonment. I guarantee that will not happen. Only through acceptance, high regard, respect, devotion, support, and safety will anyone gradually grow more secure.

# CHAPTER 4

# Becoming Experts on One Another: How to Please and Soothe Your Partner

When I see partners in a successfully maintained couple bubble, one standout feature is their ability to care for, influence, and manage one another, much the way expert parents do with their children. Both partners seem to have read and carefully studied the owner's manual for their relationship and for each other. Each is familiar with operational details that no one outside of the bubble is likely to know.

For instance, these partners know what has the most power to push the other's buttons. When the other is feeling bad, they immediately sense why. Not only that, they know how to remedy the situation. They know the right words to say, or deeds to perform, that have the power to elevate, relieve, excite, soothe, or heal each other. From a neuroscience perspective, these partners possess strong orbitofrontal cortices; well-balanced left and right brains; well-developed smart vagal systems; well-regulated breath and vocal control; and honed communication skills that keep love close and war at a far distance.

How did they get to be so adept? Are such people perhaps in possession of a perfect partner chromosome? Trust me, no. Do they have some kind of secret superpower that allows them to manage their partner emotionally? Well, maybe. As I said earlier, some of us got a better start in life than did others, with lots of positive interactions with safe adults who were interested in and curious about us. We all come to the table with primitives that don't want us to be harmed, and ambassadors that at times can be annoying. Truth is, we can be, all of us, pains in the rear. When we recite our relationship vows, perhaps we should say, "I take you as my pain in the rear, with all your history and baggage, and I take responsibility for all prior injustices you endured at the hands of those I never knew, because you now are in my care."

Hmm. How many people would be willing to say those vows? And yet, in my practice and research, that is exactly what I see couples in secure relationships doing. It is a conscious choice they make. They agree to take each other on "as is," and take responsibility for one another's care. As experts who understand their partner, they do what's necessary to relieve the other's distress or to amplify his or her elation. To many partners who find themselves at the mercy of each other's moods, this kind of expertise may indeed seem like a secret superpower they'd do almost anything to obtain.

The role of primary partner is a big one: it entails taking good care of another human pain in the rear. And the only way for this to work is for it to be fully mutual. Both partners need to become experts on one another. With this kind of arrangement, nobody really loses and everybody truly wins. You can think of it as a kind of pay-to-play version of romance, and it is, make no mistake, an investment in your future.

# THE THREE OR FOUR THINGS THAT MAKE YOUR PARTNER FEEL BAD

In fact, we all have a handful of issues with the particular power to make us feel bad. These issues typically originate during childhood, and we carry them into our adult relationships.

For instance, you may have been picked on as a child, and so you continue to feel vulnerable whenever someone tries to tease you. It affects you to this day. Or as a child, you were told you were ugly or stupid, and now you still feel you are less attractive or intelligent than others. Perhaps someone in your early childhood always had to be right, and by default always made you seem wrong. Today you continue to feel sensitive to right/wrong issues.

Here's another scenario. Let's say that during your childhood you experienced a great deal of chaos and disorganization from one or both parents. So lack of order currently upsets you, and you find yourself bothered by those who are careless, messy, and disorderly.

How many such issues does each of us actually have? Do they number in the tens? Or even more? Partners often are under the illusion that they have a vast storehouse of personal issues with which they have to deal. In my experience as a clinician, however, this is generally untrue. If we really boil our issues down to their essence, I'm willing to bet most of us will be able to identify only three or four with the power to make us feel bad. I believe most of us are disturbed by the same three or four vulnerabilities throughout our life.

Table 4.1 lists some of the main vulnerabilities I have noticed among islands and waves. Note that I'm not including anchors here. This doesn't mean they're invulnerable, or that it's unnecessary to soothe and please an anchor; however, on a daily basis, these partners are secure and their vulnerabilities are less pronounced.

### TABLE 4.1   COMMON VULNERABILITIES

| Type | Vulnerability |
|------|---------------|
| Island | Feeling intruded upon |
| | Feeling trapped, out of control |
| | Fear of too much intimacy |
| | Fear of being blamed |
| Wave | Fear of being abandoned by your partner |
| | Fear of being separated from your partner |
| | Discomfort at being alone for too long |
| | Feeling you are a burden |

# PUSHING EACH OTHER'S BUTTONS

Peggy and Simon met at a church social ten years ago. Both recently widowed, they quickly took to one another and decided to live together. Now

Simon is seventy, and Peggy sixty. Each was an only child and had a difficult childhood. Simon's mother died at childbirth, and his father gave him up for adoption. His adoptive parents divorced a year later and handed him off to his maternal grandparents, who were already burdened with financial worries. Peggy's father left when she was five, and her mother never remarried. Because her mother worked full time, Peggy went to her aunt's house after school. This aunt, who had no children, often shut Peggy in a room by herself because this aunt "needed a little peace and quiet."

The couple like to travel together, and they make frequent trips abroad. However, these often are marred by conflict. While in Europe recently, Simon lost track of Peggy at a train station. She went to get coffee, assuming Simon would wait on the train. But when she hadn't returned after five minutes, he panicked and rushed into the station to look for her.

When they finally caught up with each other, Simon was livid. "Where were you?" he shouted, as Peggy approached with two coffees.

"What's the matter?" she replied, a death glare on her face. "You're embarrassing me."

"I had no idea where you were!" Simon continued to shout. "The train's about to leave. What were you thinking?"

Peggy didn't respond. Still holding the coffees, she turned and entered the train, but a different car than the one where they had been sitting. Simon returned to his seat alone, angry and hurt that Peggy was ignoring him and unapologetic. He remained there until they reached their destination two hours later. By the time they met up on the platform, the tension between them seemed to have blown over, but the underlying issue was never discussed or resolved.

As a couple, Peggy and Simon are at the mercy of their three or four bad things. Neither is fully aware of the other's issues from childhood or of how these vulnerabilities influence them in the present. In fact, they share at least one common issue: both were abandoned during childhood. In their adult relationships, this is reflected in difficulty trusting, fear, and general insecurity. Specifically, Simon's main vulnerabilities are (1) believing he could be left at any time, (2) feeling he's the cause of other people's problems, and (3) suspecting others don't trust him. Peggy's vulnerabilities are (1) feeling she has to do everything alone, (2) believing she can't count on anyone else, and (3) feeling uncomfortable with others' expressions of emotion. By the way, from the information I've given thus far, were you able to discern that Peggy is an island, while Simon is a wave?

In the train incident, they both succeeded in pushing each other's buttons, and neither did anything to relieve the other's distress. Peggy showed insensitivity to Simon's abandonment fears by not keeping him apprised of her whereabouts, and then acting incredulous at his anger. He, on the other hand, was insensitive to her withdrawal in the face of his upset, and unprepared to relieve her (and his own) suffering by gently approaching her to make amends.

I'm not suggesting Peggy and Simon intentionally hurt one another. That's the last thing they want to do. The problem is that they don't have the benefit of being experts on one another. In the dark about each other's vulnerabilities and without the protection of a couple bubble, they continue to founder in hostile emotional territory. Their primitives have free rein much of the time, while their ambassadors remain helpless to regain the upper hand and repair the situation.

## EXERCISE: HOW ARE YOU VULNERABLE?

As an expert on your partner, you need to be familiar with the three or four things that make him or her feel bad. But, as the saying goes, "Physician, heal thyself." In other words, before attempting to identify your partner's vulnerabilities, it makes sense to have a handle on your own.

So take a minute now and think about this.

1. Sit down where you can have some private time, and think about the issues that have deeply affected you. From as early as you can remember, all the way to this point in time, what things still dog you today?

2. It may help to recall specific incidents. For example, this could be an argument with your partner in which you became very angry, or a time you felt depressed, lonely, or rejected. In each incident, what was the issue that led you to feel vulnerable?

3. Take a pen and paper (or your tablet PC) and jot down all the incidents and issues that come to mind. Don't censor yourself.

4. When you've completed your list, go back over it and look for commonalities. For example, suppose you recalled arguing with your partner after

75

he or she leaked something private about the two of you to another couple, and you also recalled being mad as a teenager when your mother said things at the dinner table you had shared privately with her. Looking at both of these now, you see the common issue was feeling betrayed. See if you can narrow your list down to three or four main vulnerabilities.

5. Focusing on your vulnerabilities might not be the most enjoyable of exercises. When you finish, do something nice for yourself (and your partner)!

# EXERCISE: HOW IS YOUR PARTNER VULNERABLE?

It is important for you to know your own vulnerabilities, and it is even more important to know your partner's. Knowing your partner's three or four bad things takes the guesswork out of what distresses him or her. Not knowing these three or four things can weaken the relationship and make it a dangerous place for both of you.

You can follow essentially the same steps as in the previous exercise. I know it might seem easier to simply ask your partner what his or her vulnerabilities are, but I'm willing to bet you're already more of an expert on your partner than you realize. So begin by compiling what you know.

1. Sit down and think about the issues that deeply affect your partner. You probably didn't know him or her during childhood, but what has your partner shared with you about that phase of life?

2. Recall specific incidents in your relationship during which you partner became distressed. In each case, what was the issue that made him or her feel vulnerable?

3. Jot down all the incidents and issues that come to mind. Don't censor yourself.

4. When you've completed your list, go back over it and look for commonalities. See if you can narrow the list down to three or four main areas of vulnerability.

5. As a final step, you may wish to check with your partner: Find out what your partner sees as the three or four things that make him or her feel bad. Watch your partner's face and listen to his or her voice for signs that these things are in fact a big deal.

Note, I have suggested doing these two exercises (identifying your own vulnerabilities and identifying your partner's vulnerabilities) on your own. Alternatively, you and your partner may choose to go through this process together.

# THE THREE OR FOUR THINGS THAT MAKE YOUR PARTNER FEEL GOOD

How many people actually know how to spontaneously make their partner feel happy and loved? I'm talking here of a phrase, a deed, or an expression aimed at one's partner meant specifically to uplift him or her. I have seen partners married for thirty years who appear dumbfounded when challenged to brighten, move, charm, or otherwise enamor one another. Yet this ability to spontaneously and predictably shift or elevate your partner's mood or emotional state is a crucial aspect of being an expert on your partner.

In my work with couples, I have found most people don't want their partner to change, not really. They fundamentally appreciate their partners as they are. But what people do want is to know how to influence, motivate, and otherwise have a positive effect on their partner. They want to avoid pushing the other's buttons. But that's not enough. They also want to know the antidotes to apply when things go awry. They want to be privy to when and where their partner has an itch, so they can scratch it for him or her.

In this way, couples seek to become competent managers of each other. In fact, their competence as partners is not unlike the competence of parents, who want to soothe their child's painful feelings and cultivate positive ones. It also can be compared to the role of a regulator. Partners who are competent managers are able to help regulate each other's moods and energy levels. As regulators, each continually monitors the other and knows when to jump in and throw a switch to help restore balance in the direction of those things that make the partner feel good.

More than just a safe environment, the couple bubble is a place for partners to feel excitement, enrichment, and most importantly, attraction. I'm not speaking here about physical attraction. Rather, I mean the kind of attraction that serves as glue to hold the relationship together. Unfortunately, fear often is the glue holding couples together. Fear may be useful for keeping a partner in line, but it obviously is counter to the notion of a couple bubble. We should *want* to be in the bubble; we shouldn't feel we *have* to be there. We want to be with our partner because there is no other place in the world we'd rather be. Our attraction is based on what we do for one another that no one else can or wants to do. Couples who don't use this kind of attraction as their glue are doomed to fail sooner or later.

# EXERCISE: WHAT CAN UPLIFT YOUR PARTNER?

Are you aware of what things you can say or do that have the power to relieve distress and uplift your partner? Take a minute and think about these now.

1. You may find it helpful to begin with the list of vulnerabilities you made earlier. For each of the three or four things that make your partner feel bad, you probably can identify something that will mollify the bad feeling. For instance, if my history has me doubting my worth as a parent, my partner can predictably brighten my mood with a spontaneous "You're such a good father," delivered right into my eyes.

2. Check the list you come up with against the antidotes in table 4.2, which might give you additional ideas.

3. You may also want to create a list of the things your partner can (and does) do that please and uplift you. If you are doing this exercise together, you can create separate lists for each other and then compare notes.

# SCRATCHING YOUR PARTNER'S ITCH

Remember how ineffective Peggy and Simon were at handling their respective vulnerabilities? Well, as it turns out, they're not much better at making each other feel good.

As a child, Peggy received positive messages about her prettiness, and she's always felt good about her appearance. She has questioned her intelligence, however, ever since a teacher humiliated her in grade school. Although Peggy completed college, she viewed herself as an average student. Simon, on the other hand, has always considered himself intelligent. Despite his difficult upbringing, he managed to put himself through college and earned a degree in chemical engineering. He doesn't believe, however, that he is lovable and worthwhile as a human being. He never felt truly wanted, and now he continually anticipates that Peggy will leave him.

Throughout their European vacation, Simon told Peggy how beautiful she is and how attracted to her he is. Yet he wondered why she often failed to respond to his compliments and physical advances. He figured if he just repeated them more often, she would be more appreciative. But that didn't seem to work.

Peggy is the one who handles the couple's travel arrangements. Although Simon is aware of her doubts about her intelligence, he never employs that knowledge by saying, "You're so smart" or "I love that you know the history of this place" or "I always learn so much being with you." If he expressed any variation of these messages, he might enjoy a brightening in her face that he never sees when commenting on her beauty. This might lead to a mutual amplification of positive feeling, as her brightening causes his face to brighten. But alas, because he doesn't use this approach, he gets zilch, zippo, nada.

Peggy, on the other hand, sings Simon's praises when it comes to his smarts. She truly values his intelligence and is surprised when the most her comments get out of him is a social smile. If, however, she looked into his eyes and said, "You are a good man" or "You're the one I've been waiting for" or "I love that you want to keep me close" or "I will never leave you," she might find Simon responsive in ways that benefit her, as well.

Peggy and Simon lose out on the advantages of a couple bubble—both the safety and security that come with mutual protection and distress relief, and the vitality and attractiveness that come with providing the missing self-esteem pieces from childhood. As partners, each holds the keys to the other's self-esteem and self-worth. Remember, as we discussed in chapter 1, self-esteem and self-worth are developed through our contact with other people. You misunderstand if you think these goods are provided by the self. They're not; they're provided by the other. That's how it works and that's how it has always worked, starting from infancy.

Now I'd like you to meet another couple.

Paul and Barbara have become very social since their last child left the nest two years ago. They like going out with friends and enjoy participating in community and philanthropic activities. Barbara was abandoned by her father when she was four; her mother, who raised her and her older sister alone, passed away last year. Barbara is still sad about the loss of her mother and of her children, who are all away at school. Paul was the oldest of five siblings, all male. His father was especially hard on him during childhood. His mother tended to take a back seat to his father's authoritarianism.

Although this couple's vulnerabilities are not dissimilar from those of Peggy and Simon, they respond to one another in a very different manner. Paul understands Barbara's history, and is able to help her recognize when her reactions to him are influenced by the childhood loss of her father. Whenever Barbara pulls away from him, Paul knows what to do to be of help. Likewise, Barbara understands Paul's history; she stands ready whenever his insecurities and perfectionism arise and knows what to do to help him.

For example, on the way home from a dinner event one evening, Paul noticed that Barbara, sitting next to him in the passenger seat, was unusually quiet. He remembered that, during dinner, a woman at their table had talked about caring for her aging parents. Guessing Barbara was still thinking about this, he said softly, "You're remembering your mother, aren't you?"

She nodded and wiped away a stray tear.

Paul could feel her distress. Reaching for her hand and kissing it, he said, "I'm so sorry, honey. I know you miss her."

Wiping away more tears, she whispered, "Thank you."

Paul was tracking Barbara that night, as he does whenever they are together. He knows what can hurt her, how she displays that hurt, and what he can do to help. He knows there are only three or four things that consistently have the power to hurt Barbara, and these vulnerabilities have existed since childhood and will probably exist until the day she dies. He doesn't need to ask Barbara, "What's wrong?" He already knows what's bothering her. So he guesses; after all, it couldn't be a hundred possible things, or even a dozen. She is predictable, as is he, so both of them use their knowledge of one another to be of help.

Asking a partner, "What's wrong?" is a bit like asking "Who are you, again?" As partners, we should know. Others may not know and are not required to know, but we most certainly are. That's our job, and that's why we're paid the big bucks! We do for our partners what others would not want to do because they don't really care.

Of course, our guesses will not be correct a hundred percent of the time. I'm not suggesting you need to be clairvoyant. It is possible, for instance, that Barbara's thoughts had moved to an event earlier in the day, perhaps something she was about to share with her husband. In that case, no harm would have come from Paul's incorrect guess; the couple simply would have shifted to the new topic.

Barbara believes she is unable to handle loss, despite the fact that she has survived many losses in her life. She has always seen herself as less attractive than her older sister, who was surrounded by boyfriends; in contrast, Barbara excelled in academics. Although she knows better as an adult, the child part of her still believes she was responsible for her father leaving because she had disappointed him. This has made the transition of their children from home to college even more difficult than it might otherwise have been.

Paul regularly makes use of his knowledge about Barbara's missing pieces and doesn't spend much effort on things that have little or no effect on her self-esteem. He frequently tells her how proud he is of her as a mother and how lucky he feels to be with her. He repeatedly reminds her, "Honey, I'm with you for the long haul." He never misses an opportunity to look at her as if she is the most beautiful, sexy woman on the planet and tells her so, as well. These three or four things that he provides not only help heal the past, but also give her what she most needs in the present. He loves that he is able to move her emotionally. He scratches the right itch each time.

Because of his neglect issues from childhood, Paul needs to know he is trusted and trustworthy. He doubts himself to such a degree that he sometimes becomes frozen and unable to stick by decisions. He needs to hear that his opinion is respected, although he has a way of undercutting that support by suspecting that anyone who always agrees with him is weak minded.

Barbara makes liberal use of her knowledge about Paul's missing pieces and avoids pandering to the things that don't matter that much to him. She often tells him, "I trust you with my life." She never argues with him just to prove herself right, but will stand up to him when she believes doing so is important for both of them. She regularly tells Paul how much she believes in his ability to do the right thing, and to fix it if he discovers otherwise. Barbara knows what Paul needs to shore up his self-esteem and self-worth, and she does it without hesitation because it benefits her, as well.

Barbara and Paul maintain a loving couple bubble. As experts on one another, they can detect when the other has an itch, and they know exactly how to scratch it to provide relief. Often it takes just a smile or a look or a grasp of the hand to calm each other's primitives and communicate the support that is needed. They get their needs met in ways that would not be possible if each were alone; they do this for each other because they can and because it makes them more attractive—and even indispensible—to one another. Nor does anyone outside their bubble do what they do for one another, and as such, their world is a safer, more protective world than the one that exists outside their bubble.

---

# EXERCISE: THE EMOTE ME GAME

You can play this game with your partner, each taking turns to "emote" the other. Or you can practice it without telling your partner what you're doing. Either way, you stand to learn a lot about your relationship.

1. Say or do something to make your partner smile brightly. Drawing upon your knowledge of your partner, try to anticipate what will bring a smile to his or her face, then watch and see if it works. For example, you might give your partner a back rub or relate a special shared memory.

2. Now say something complimentary about your partner that will profoundly move him or her. You will know you have succeeded if you bring tears to your partner's eyes. I don't mean tears of sadness, but the moistness that comes when we feel deeply touched. Brief, declarative statements are most likely to succeed. Long, drawn-out statements will fail. Avoid adding qualifications. For example, your partner may be moved if you say, "You're

the most trustworthy person I know," but saying "You're a very trustworthy person...most of the time" is unlikely to produce the desired effect. Neither will a lazy compliment, such as "You know how much I like your cooking." That isn't very moving if you're just repeating what you think your partner already knows. And don't always expect Immediate results. If your partner doesn't respond to a compliment, take that as information about what affects him or her, and try something else.

3. Finally, say or do something that causes your partner to get excited. You can see excitement in the eyes: they widen and the pupils dilate, if only for an instant. Your partner's face may become redder, and his or her vocal tone may become higher in pitch and louder.

4. In each case (whether you're finding a way to make your partner smile, complimenting him or her, or exciting him or her), if you are playing this game together, don't ask your partner what will work. It's your job as the expert to find this out. And don't ask your partner if what you said or did worked, either. Look for the clues; notice your partner's reaction. Through this process, you build your expertise. And your partner does the same. You will both receive benefits. Remember, you are wired together!

The two of you can play the Emote Me Game whenever you feel like it. Experiment with different positive effects: make your partner relax, make your partner laugh, or anything else you can think of.

# FOURTH GUIDING PRINCIPLE

The fourth principle in this book is that *partners who are experts on one another know how to please and soothe each other.* This means becoming familiar with your partner's primary vulnerabilities and knowing the antidotes that are effective for each. Table 4.2 summarizes some of the typical vulnerabilities for islands and waves we have seen in this chapter and offers suggestions for helping your partner minimize these when they make an appearance. Again, I haven't included anchors because they tend to be secure and less in need of antidotes.

## TABLE 4.2 WHAT YOU CAN DO TO
## HELP YOUR PARTNER

| Vulnerability—what bothers your partner | Antidote—what to do or say to your partner |
|---|---|
| Islands | |
| Feeling intruded upon | Approach quietly, rather than calling your partner by name. |
| | If your partner is busy, say, "I need to talk with you in a couple minutes," and then leave. |
| | "Let me know when you're ready. If it's more than _____ minutes, I'll start and you can join in." |
| Feeling trapped, out of control | "I need a few minutes of your time, and then you can get back to what you're doing." |
| | "I can see you've had enough. Run along and we'll continue later." |
| | "You have a couple of choices here." |
| Fear of too much intimacy | Pay attention to the level of intimacy with which your partner is comfortable. Ease into closeness. |
| | "Do you want me to stop?" |
| | "Is this annoying you?" |
| Fear of being blamed | "I so appreciate what you did, but you were out of line in this case." |
| | "I understand why you did what you did. Your heart was in the right place." |
| | "Look, it's not [all] your fault. And if it were, that wouldn't matter to me." |

| Waves | |
|---|---|
| Fear of being abandoned by you | "Don't worry, I'm not going anywhere. You couldn't get rid of me if you wanted to."<br><br>"Please stay close to me. I want to be in close contact today."<br><br>"You are my tether." |
| Being separated from you | Make use of technology, such as text messaging. Nothing elaborate, just "hi" or "loving you" or "ugh, bad meeting" or any pithy comment that suggests "I'm thinking about you." |
| Discomfort being alone for too long | "I'm looking forward to our dinner together tonight. I can't wait to hear about your day."<br><br>"Call me if you need to talk."<br><br>"I promise I'll call you as soon as we land, even if it's late." |
| Feeling he or she is a burden | "You're no more of a burden to me than I am to you!"<br><br>"I love that we know exactly what to do to take care of each other."<br><br>"You are one burden I'll always enjoy carrying." |

Here are some supporting principles to guide you in soothing and pleasing your partner:

1. Learn to rapidly repair damage. Being an expert on your partner means you are continually alert to his or her mood and feelings. If your partner is bothered, you know it immediately. It doesn't matter whether your partner is bothered because of something occurring between the two of you or because of something outside the relationship. In either

case, you are enough of an expert that you can speedily make an educated guess about which of his or her three or four bad things has been touched off. There is no reason to let any problems fester. Seeing your partner in distress should be the signal to "stop the presses" before continuing on with *anything*.

For example, if you think you caused your partner pain, you might say, "That didn't go well, did it?" or "I'm so sorry. Did that just hurt you?" The worst thing you can do is ignore what you see on your partner's face or hear in your partner's voice. Let your partner know he or she can count on you to step up and say or do whatever is needed to repair the damage.

And the same applies to you. You can rely on your partner to be there for you, to know your vulnerabilities and soothe you when you're upset. It's as though when you formed your relationship, you took out a policy that would ensure your comfort, and now because you've kept up with your premiums (that is, by being there for your partner), you're able to relax and cash in whenever something seems to have gotten out of hand.

2. Prevent problems before they arise. Knowing how to repair damage is helpful, but it is even better to anticipate and avoid difficulties. Of course, it won't be possible to avert all challenges. Life doesn't work that way. But as experts, there is a lot you and your partner can do to please and keep each other happy. Rather than waiting until you see trouble brewing, be proactive with your partner. Make a habit of saying and doing the things that make him or her feel good. Don't assume your partner already knows how much you love him or her; don't figure you've already adequately expressed everything you appreciate about your partner. Find new and creative ways to convey the three or four things that make your partner feel good. In this way, you make deposits you can draw on when the going gets rough.

3. You may be wondering, what if my partner and I disagree about what our three or four bad things and three or four good things are? The answer is that it doesn't really matter. It isn't actually critical that you correctly identify your own three or four things or know how to scratch

your own itch. What's important is that you know how to do these things with your partner, and vice versa.

So, how do you know if what you've come up with for your partner really works? The proof, so to speak, is in the pudding. The evidence will always be visible on your partner's face, audible in his or her voice, or apparent in his or her spontaneous shift in mood.

There's no need to get into a debate with your partner about what your three or four things are (bad or good). That's why I referred to this expertise as a "secret" superpower. Simply respond according to what you understand these good and bad things to be, then sit back and watch the results. If it turns out you're not seeing the desired results, chances are you are not yet scratching the right itch. In that case, it's time to go back to the drawing board and learn more about your partner. Through a process of experimentation, of trial and error, you can continue to become a better expert.

# CHAPTER 5

# Launchings and Landings: How to Use Morning and Bedtime Rituals

B reakfast in bed. The thrill of birthday and Christmas mornings. Wake-up songs. Wake-up kisses. Perhaps these are some familiar snapshots from your childhood morning rituals. Bedtime stories. Lullabies. Daily debriefings. Being tucked into bed at night. Prayers. Kisses on the forehead. These are all bedtime rituals.

From our earliest beginnings throughout our adult life, we must transition from sleep to wake, and from wake to sleep. We must launch in the morning, and land at night. We learn this during childhood, and the habits we form tend to stay with us. The manner in which we are accustomed to shifting between consciousness and unconsciousness has important consequences for our mental and physical health, as well as for the health of our relationship.

In fact, many people—both singles and couples—have trouble with mornings and nighttimes. Depressed people are sometimes more depressed upon awakening. Facing a new day, especially after a nighttime of upsetting dreams, a person who is depressed may feel unmotivated and fearful and dread getting up. Anxious people are sometimes more anxious at night. While lying in bed, worrisome thoughts, images, and memories tend to fill their mind with vexing internal chatter. The transition between wake and sleep can be so painful for some people that they prefer to simply fall into bed, pass out, and not deal with it at all.

If your partner has any of these troubles, he or she may have sought relief through medication. And for some, this is effective. However, sleeping medications can be addictive or lead to other negative results: difficulty waking; depression; next-day grogginess; rebound insomnia, and even drunken, out-of-control behavior. Worse yet, your partner may be tempted to seek relief through self-medicating activities and substances, such as pornography, chat rooms, online poker, late-night television, alcohol, food, marijuana, or a combination of the aforementioned.

So why have I included a chapter on morning and nighttime rituals as part of this owner's manual for your partner? Because you can and should be your partner's best antidepressant and antianxiety agent. And best of all, no insurance reimbursement needed!

As we saw in chapter 4, being an expert on your partner means you know how to please and soothe him or her whenever needed. During infancy, hopefully this kind of soothing was provided by a primary caregiver. If your partner is an anchor, he or she had a secure base from which to explore the environment and return whenever in need of comfort and refueling. If your partner is an island, however, that secure base was relatively unavailable, and now he or she may deny or dismiss the need for a partner to soothe and be there as a source of comfort. After all, why consider the importance of such security if it was never available in the first place?

Studies of children in Israeli kibbutzim, where communal living arrangements meant they were separated at nighttime and early mornings from their mother, give us insight into this question. Attachment theorist John Bowlby (1969) predicted children in such situations would be less secure, and researchers have documented this to be the case. For example, Abraham Sagi and colleagues (1994), who compared children who slept at home with children who slept away from their parents, found that if the parent was consistently unavailable at bedtime, the child was more likely to be insecure. More recently, Liat Tikotsky and her team (2010) reported that parents who experienced communal living as infants were more like to report concerns about their infant's sleep disturbances. Their study revealed a silver lining, however: these parents also were more likely to soothe their infants at bedtime.

Whether or not your partner felt smoothly transitioned at bedtime and in the morning during childhood, here's the good news: your partner has the perfect opportunity now to have that secure base again, or for the very first time…with you!

# SLEEPING AND WAKING SEPARATELY

Noah and Isabella, both in their mid thirties, are raising two young children while working hard at their respective professions. In the early years of marriage, they used to go out together and keep late hours. Now, with child-rearing duties and a mounting financial burden, both are too busy and too exhausted. They have enlisted extended family members to help with various daycare duties, and have a young babysitter on nights when both work late.

When she can, Isabella prefers to go to bed around 9 p.m., as soon as the children are asleep. Noah has always been a night owl, and stays up until at least midnight. Isabella is the only one up early enough to make the children's breakfast. After that, she runs off to the gym and then to work. Noah typically wakes an hour after she has left the house. They maintain their disparate sleep-wake patterns on weekends, as well.

These partners have become unhappy with one another. Both blame their dissatisfaction on the children, their work, and their financial woes. Noah has become increasingly depressed and anxious, and Isabella is resentful of his complaining. Neither looks to their lack of togetherness at bedtime and waking as a problem. Yet each complains of waning energy, powerlessness, and a growing sense of hopelessness about the marriage.

What effect do you think Isabella going to bed early has on Noah? What effect does the sight of an empty bed have on Isabella when she briefly wakes at 1 a.m.? What effect does waking alone in the morning have on both partners?

When living alone, we may not be bothered by the sight of an empty bed. However, when we live with a partner, we become accustomed to having him or her next to us—preferably awake while we are awake, and asleep while we are asleep. Whether we are aware of it or not, we may react to an empty bed when we expect someone to be there. Even if we know it is only a temporary separation, the experience that our partner has left us can be unsettling.

Isabella has island qualities and appreciates her time alone, yet she sometimes finds it hard to fall back to sleep after waking to find Noah still up. And Noah, who has wave tendencies, sometimes feels abandoned when Isabella goes to bed before he does, even though he is naturally a night owl.

To complicate matters, their respective genders may influence Isabella's and Noah's sleep experience. In fact, various studies have shown that men and women not only have different sleep patterns, but perceive their experience differently. For example, John Dittami and colleagues (2007) compared couples when they slept alone and when they slept together over a period of twenty eight nights. They found that women had more disrupted sleep when they were with a partner than when they slept alone, while men reported enjoying sleeping together more than women did.

Wendy Troxel (2010) pointed out a paradox emerging from this field of research. On the one hand, measures of the biophysiological changes that occur during sleep (e.g., reaching the most restful level of sleep—called level 4 sleep; having fewer body movements) indicate that, overall, couples sleep better alone. On the other hand, couples subjectively report that they sleep better when they are together. She theorizes that, for both men and women, the need to feel secure at night outweighs any sleep disturbances that may accompany cosleeping. This would explain, for instance, why Isabella is disturbed when she wakes to an empty bed. It also supports what I stress in the guiding principles of this book: the importance of keeping your partner safe and secure.

It's also possible that Isabella and Noah are influenced by their respective circadian rhythms—the daily biological cycle that determines when an individual is inclined to eat, sleep, and perform other actions. Research has shown that couples with different rhythms, such as night owls paired with early birds, can experience instability in their relationships. For example, Jeffry Larson and team (Larson, Crane, and Smith 1991) found that couples with different night and morning orientations had more arguments than did similarly oriented couples, and spent less quality time together. It's actually common for couples to have different daily rhythms, yet I believe it's possible and even healthy for these partners to get onto the same sleep schedule, or at least to create ways to begin and end the day together. You can improve your relationship if you make the effort to coordinate sleep/wake patterns with your partner.

# SLEEPING AND WAKING TOGETHER

In my experience as a couple therapist, partners who routinely make plans to meet each other in bed at night or to put one another to bed (whether or not they cosleep) and who routinely wake together report much more relationship satisfaction than couples who do not. Let's look at some examples of how this can work.

## TRANSITIONING IN SYNC

Rebecca and Vince are in their mid thirties and have two young children. Similar to Noah and Isabella, both are hardworking, pulling a dual income to keep up with a mortgage, huge health insurance premiums, and other expenses that keep them worried about the future. Unlike Noah and Isabella, they don't have extended family to help out, and they can't afford daycare or babysitters. Rebecca works out of the home, and Vince works at an office six out of seven days. Prior to marriage, Rebecca was more of a wave and Vince more of an island. However, within a couple years of marriage, their secure, skillful way of relating helped them both become anchors.

Despite their stressful lives, the couple are resolute about nighttime and morning rituals, both for the children and for themselves. They work together to put the children to bed, and afterward enjoy watching television, talking quietly about their day, or making love. Although Rebecca often is tempted to step into her home office to check for late-night e-mails, she resists unless a crisis is occurring in her work. When this does happen on occasion, Vince is understanding and usually makes a point of waiting up for her. About once a week, Vince has to get up extra early for a meeting at work. Rebecca likes to get up with him, even though she doesn't need to and he hasn't asked her to, so they can share a cup of coffee before he leaves. She finds she appreciates the early start on her own work day. At other times, she forgoes the coffee and heads back to bed for another hour after he leaves.

Rebecca and Vince often lie quietly in bed just before sleep, gazing into one another's eyes and then gently sending one another off to sleep. At other times, they take turns reading to one another each night, and alternate selecting the books they will enjoy together. They like to create and experiment with new bedtime rituals, as well. For instance, for a while they made a point every night after turning out the lights to express their gratitude. They thought of all the people who had touched their lives, both living and dead, naming them one by one and wishing each well. Sometimes either Rebecca or Vince fell asleep before finishing the list. No matter. Both saw this ritual as a way to transition into sleep, and they liked that it helped them feel connected not only to one another, but also to the people in their lives.

The couple awaken together and always make a point of lounging together for several minutes before taking care of their morning chores, including waking the children. Sometimes they gaze into one another's eyes upon waking, as they did prior to sleeping. Even though their days are busy, both feel energized by their time together at these crucial transitioning periods, and feel connected and hopeful about their day apart. They launch each other into the day and land together into the night.

## EARLY BIRDS AND NIGHT OWLS

Things are relatively easy for Rebecca and Vince because their rhythms are naturally similar and easily in sync. But what about couples with conflicting rhythms? It may require more effort and compromise, but such couples also can benefit from shared rituals.

Carrie and Marcia have opposite sleep patterns. Carrie is a night owl, and Marcia is an early bird. Carrie admits she is an island and always has been. She also believes, and is probably correct, that Marcia is an anchor.

Marcia worries about Carrie and her health. She notices how overtired she is during the day and that she tends to eat high-carb foods right before going to sleep. Carrie insists these habits suit her well, although she would rather Marcia stay up with her and watch TV. Marcia's internal clock doesn't allow her to stay up; she starts to fall asleep almost precisely at 9:30 every night. Marcia also doesn't like to be woken at night, and she begs Carrie to be quieter when she comes into the room after Marcia has fallen asleep.

Carrie sometimes gets irritated that Marcia can't stand sound or light in the room at night. Carrie wants to be next to Marcia at night, and would prefer to turn on a small nightlight and read whenever she has trouble sleeping. But out of concern for Marcia, she avoids doing that. Instead, Carrie made it her habit to slip out of bed, tiptoe out the door, and look for other activities downstairs. She might check online social network sites; eat fatty foods, particularly ice cream, which she adores; or watch movies into the wee hours of the night. Often when she finally went back to bed, Carrie would feel anxious and disappointed in herself.

Then one night, by chance, Carrie discovered something interesting. She was extremely tired after participating in a company sports event and went to bed early—even before Marcia. Marcia finished her normal bedtime routine and went to bed half an hour after Carrie. As she fell asleep, she gently stroked Carrie's back. The next morning, Carrie awoke refreshed and noticed she had not woken up during the night. As an experiment, she tried going to bed early again later that week, with the same results. Having fallen asleep before Marcia, while in bed with Marcia she was able to sleep through the night, without late-night eating or television watching or any of the other activities she later regretted.

Carrie's late night activities had developed because, without realizing it, she felt abandoned by Marcia. It hadn't occurred to Marcia that Carrie needed to be put to bed. Marcia had good sleep habits from childhood, such as going to bed at a similar time each night and getting a full eight hours of sleep, but Carrie did not. Despite Carrie's lifetime as a night owl, she became a con-verted early bird. As an added bonus, both Carrie and Marcia could enjoy the mornings together. Moreover, Carrie started working out before going to work, and lost weight because she was no longer snacking at night. Sleeping together and waking together brought Marcia and Carrie closer than they were before.

Early birds often come from families of early birds, and night owls tend to come from night owl families. Their respective clocks were set during infancy according to their mother's clock. Nevertheless, it is not impossible to train themselves to switch species, or at least to meet one another midway, espe-cially when the future of their relationship is at stake. Training can include several days of light exposure at night for the early bird, and several days of light exposure in the early morning for the night owl; in other words, give your partner a little time to adjust to either staying up longer or getting up earlier before you expect him or her to be fully functional during those times.

Partners who wish to forego the effort to change their internal clock can simply accept one another as night owls and early birds, and use this differ-ence for their mutual benefit. For instance, the night owl is more productive at nighttime and can perform mutually beneficial tasks, such as the family bookkeeping or preparing school lunches for the kids, at night. Likewise, the early bird has more energy during the morning hours and can take on some of the couple's morning tasks, such as driving the kids to school. Even so, night owl / early bird couples can, and should, open and close their days together with simple rituals.

## EXERCISE: A WEEK OF RITUAL

Set aside a week during which you can experiment with creative launchings and landings. Make sure your partner is on board with the idea. You can say that you will be taking the lead, and all he or she needs to do is be available, sit back, and enjoy the ride.

Here's how it works.

1. You can select any week of the year as your ritual week. However, you may want to avoid a week during which one of you has a business trip scheduled or another atypical event that might interfere. Choosing an average week will make it easier to subsequently apply what you discover.

2. During the week, land and launch together. Think about what your partner might enjoy. Perhaps include some activities that will be new to you as a couple. I've suggested a variety of rituals in this chapter that you may want to try. But please don't be limited by my suggestions. Get creative!

3. Let each ritual be a surprise to your partner. Sometimes the element of surprise adds fun and excitement to a relationship.

4. At the end of the ritual week, compare your experiences. Which rituals did you each like? And why? What did you learn about yourself and each other? Decide together which rituals you would like to incorporate into your relationship on an ongoing basis.

Approach this as an experiment, but without critiquing each other. Pay attention to how each ritual affects both of you. Better sleep? Better dreams? Better day?

# SEPARATIONS AND REUNIONS: ANOTHER KIND OF LAUNCHING AND LANDING

In addition to the act of waking up each morning, separating from your partner—whether to go to work, school, or wherever—can be thought of as a type of launching. You and your partner launch each other away from the relationship and into the nonrelationship world. How you do this can affect the amount of energy, confidence, and support you feel while you are away dealing with your parents, your coworkers, your kids, a job interview, a college final, and so on.

Similarly, much like going to sleep at night, reuniting with your partner after a separation, even a brief one, is a type of landing. It represents your return home. Remember, the couple bubble *is* home. Home *is* the partnership. How you land and reunite affects the couple bubble and each other's well-being in the home.

How are launchings and landings handled in your relationship? At the moment of separation, do you embrace your partner for longer than a second? Do you gaze into your partner's eyes? Or perhaps you simply run out the door. After the separation, when you reunite, do you embrace and gaze briefly into your partner's eyes. Or do you take the reunion for granted and carry on as if the two of you hadn't been apart at all?

Remember Noah and Isabella, who did not share morning and evening rituals? Because she is an island, Isabella doesn't feel she has missed anything when she leaves in the morning without a proper launching ritual. Noah, on the other hand, complains about feeling listless while at work and lacks confidence in his interactions with others.

When Noah picks Isabella up at the airport, he grabs her luggage and races to the car; then they hurry home. He makes no effort to spend time face to face with his partner. Her airplane may have landed, but she and he have not. Because this couple don't reunite properly, they inevitably fight in the car. It doesn't matter what the fight is about; the truth is that it is a consequence of failing to attune to one another upon reunion. You might argue that they have something to argue about, and that's why they fight. But I would remind you that our primitives respond to threat cues faster than we can determine whether the threat is real. In this case, the threat is simply the failure to take the time to re-attune after a separation. We aren't talking about large amounts of time. If Noah were to initiate a few minutes of together time, I guarantee they could save themselves hours of fighting.

Now remember Rebecca and Vince, who enjoy morning and evening rituals. These two also pay close attention to their separations and reunions. For example, they do what I call the Welcome Home Ritual. When either returns home at any time of day or night, both seek each other out before performing any other tasks. They greet each other before greeting the children, pets, or guests in the house. They embrace and hold each other until each feels the other relax. Because it's easier to feel tension in a partner's body than in one's own body, they use this to their advantage. Rebecca points out to Vince any places of tension she detects upon greeting him so he can make an effort to release them. Vince does the same for her. Only after completing their welcome ritual do they go about their business. Not only they, but everyone in the household benefits from their attunement.

I have seen many couples diffuse or resolve many conflicts by simply taking seriously the need for launching and landing rituals. We take too much for granted when it comes to separations and reunions, and pay the price for not understanding the natural human imperative to make and continually remake secure connections with our most important others. Don't take my word for this. Check your own launchings and landings. Play with them. Perform them properly, and then improperly or not at all. Compare the difference. Experience for yourself.

## EXERCISE: THE WELCOME HOME RITUAL

Today (or tomorrow) when your partner comes home from work, take the time to fully greet him or her. If you look into each other's eyes, keep looking until each of you can see your partner's eyes focus and soften. Don't stop until you see that happen! If you embrace, don't let go until you feel the other fully relax. No skimping permitted. It's not a timed event.

Notice how you feel after this brief ritual. Is your household more peaceful? I'll be surprised if you don't find everyone, not just the two of you, benefits: the kids, the dog, the cat, even the fish!

# FIFTH GUIDING PRINCIPLE

The fifth principle of this book is that *partners with busy lives should create and use bedtime and morning rituals, as well as reunion rituals, to stay connected.*

As I've stated, this book is less about helping yourself and more about helping your partner. Of course, in a truly mutual relationship, your needs will be met, as well, because both of you will take care of one another. However, the burden for finding opportunities to take care of your partner rests upon you. Two such opportunities are available each day: one at bedtime and the other upon rising in the morning.

Here are some supporting principles to guide you as you develop launching and landing rituals:

1. You both benefit when you put your partner to bed. Although going to sleep together every night would be nice, that isn't always feasible. One or the other of you may have work to do on a given night. Or, as we discussed, one of you may be a night owl. Nevertheless, you can find the time to put your partner to bed. Make this a habit. And take turns on different nights so both of you have the experience of being put to bed.

2. Variety is the spice of ritual. Create lots of bedtime and morning rituals for yourselves. For example, sometimes you may like to watch a TV program or movie together, as a way to wind down from the day. Of course, this easily can become an isolating activity (islands, I'm talking to you). Don't let that happen. Be sure to make contact at regular intervals during the program or movie. Talk about it (you're not in a movie theater, so don't worry about disturbing anyone else). Look at your partner during emotional, funny, or stupid moments. Hold hands.

   Other suggestions for bedtime rituals include:

   a. Listen to an audio book or a podcast. Or the good old-fashioned radio. Turn the lights out, hold hands, and listen together.

   b. Pray together. (No religion required.)

   c. Spend time quietly gazing into your partner's eyes. It can be playful and fun. It can also be relaxing.

d. Read to your partner. When was the last time someone read to you or you read to someone? Caution: reading to your partner can put him or her to sleep, so if that's not your intent, consider choosing something else to do.

e. Tickle your partner's back, draw pictures on your partner's back, or play the "guess what word I'm writing on your back" game. Do this in the dark so it's a bedtime transition.

f. Give your partner an orgasm. It's good for health and for the relationship. Your partner having an orgasm can give you a contact high. Endorphins, oxytocin, and vasopressin flow into both partners' bloodstreams, making you feel connected. Orgasms also are a great muscle relaxant and antianxiety remedy.

Suggestions for morning rituals include:

a. Make breakfast (in bed, or not) for your partner. Alternatively, you can go out for breakfast or to a favorite coffee or tea shop.

b. Lie in bed together and gaze into your partner's eyes. Greet your partner with a loving "Good morning!"

c. Quietly talk with your partner about the day and what each of you will be doing, facing, or accomplishing. Use this time to remind one another of tasks, appointments, or agreements concerning this day only. Make plans for the nighttime. Agree to meet in bed at a certain time.

d. Give each other orgasms. This can work especially well as part of your morning and evening rituals if you and your partner have opposing sexual arousal patterns ("I want sex at night, and he wants it in the morning"). This way each gets what he or she wants.

5. Wherever one goes, the other goes. For partners who share a couple bubble, this is true emotionally, even when it isn't always the case physically. It's kind of like running a three-legged race: if one person falls, the other can't go anywhere. So you want to work as a team and hold each other up. When it comes time to separate, whether for the

day or a longer trip, make certain to give your partner a proper send-off. Make eye contact, embrace, make reaffirming remarks about your feelings for one another, and do whatever else it takes to fill your partner's tank to the brim. You want him or her to perform at his or her peak.

# CHAPTER 6

# The Go-To People: How to Remain Available to One Another

Marsha and Brian have been together for twelve years. Intentionally childless, they committed themselves to their respective careers and to standing in as the best possible surrogate parents to their nieces and nephews whenever necessary. By all accounts, Marsha and Brian are very much in love. But one problem has been brewing since they first met: both Brian and Marsha retain their own counsel in the form of friends, colleagues, and even on occasion separate psychotherapists. Both are accustomed to going to others outside their couple bubble for the purpose of sharing intimate details about themselves, and neither serves as the primary go-to person for the other. Both have had their secrets, and both have spread information to which the other was not privy. Neither sees any problem with this.

One night as they're sitting down to dinner, Marsha turns to her husband and says, "Who is the girl I saw you with on that social networking site?"

Brian looks up, surprised. "What girl?"

Marsha eats two mouthfuls of salad before she replies. "I saw a tagged photo of you with this woman on my friend's page," she says nonchalantly. "You had a green plastic cup in your hand, and your arm was around her. Look, I don't care. I just want to know."

Brian sets his fork down. "I didn't even know you were into social networking. You looked at your friend's page? That means *you* have a page on that site."

"I do," Marsha acknowledges. "You don't have to know everything about me, do you?"

"Nope," says Brain. "You're right, I don't."

They eat in silence for a few moments. "So," says Marsha, "who's that woman?"

Brian gives a short laugh. "You don't have to know everything about me, either," he says, "do you?"

For a second Marsha looks taken aback. Then she joins his laugh. And the issue is dropped…at least for the time being.

## THE BENEFITS OF FEELING TETHERED TO ANOTHER PERSON

But as I mentioned, trouble has been brewing for Brian and Marsha. It finally surfaces after she loses her job as VP of marketing during an economic downturn. Suddenly the life she seemingly breezed through is filled with uncertainty. She finds herself second-guessing her career choices, relationship security, even the decision not to have children. Talking with her usual circle of friends doesn't provide the level of support she needs. Perhaps the worst part is that, for the first time, Marsha and Brian find themselves constantly quibbling.

"I feel like I can't talk to you," she says. "I can talk to my sisters and my best friends. Why not you?"

One answer to Marsha's plea might be the simple difference that Brian is Marsha's primary attachment partner. This makes him "deep family" in a way others are not. If Marsha were to marry one of her best friends, we would quickly find out if she could still talk as easily as she would like. Things change when a person is elevated to primary attachment status. However, it could also be that Brian himself makes it difficult for her to talk to him.

"Of course you can talk to me," says Brian with as much sincerity as he can muster. "You can talk to me about pretty much anything."

"So then why don't you tell me stuff about yourself?" counters Marsha, putting aside her own pressing issues for the moment. "I know you keep things from me—things you tell your best buddies."

"Well, there are certain things I like to keep private. I think you should keep things private, too. I think it would be boring if people were completely open books."

We therapists keep an ear out for comments such as Brian's. His notion of things being kept private reveals his one-person or pro-self model of relationships, which is characteristic of islands and waves. For the past twelve years, Marsha has been comfortable with that, too. But now her own personal crisis is pushing her to seek another way of relating within her marriage.

"Why can't I know the same things your friends know?" Marsha persists.

"They understand things you just wouldn't understand," replies Brian. "They're guys, for Pete's sake!"

"I don't get it," says Marsha, shaking her head.

"There you go. I rest my case," laughs Brian. "You just don't get it."

What this couple lacks is the means to create for themselves a consistent sense of security—a feeling of being tethered to one another, of having a secure base from which to launch and land. By tethered, I mean connected in such a way that—as with a blankie, a warm glass of milk, or a teddy bear—we feel a level of comfort and security that can get us through our days and nights. Marsha and Brian do not share this kind of secure connection. They don't benefit from the protection of a couple bubble, and although they occasionally give lip service to the notion of "you can always talk to me," in reality they aren't free to go to one another about anything and everything that might be on their minds.

## WHAT MATTERS MOST

To be sure, most of us begin to realize the need to be tethered to at least one other person, if not early in life, then eventually as we near death. A mentor of mine once told me that people near death never talk about wishing they had traveled to this place or that, or made this amount of money. Their lament, if any, was about their relationships. Many wished they had said they were sorry, or told someone they loved him or her, or just been able to feel closer. So if you're among the skeptics when it comes to committed relationships, I challenge you to interview people who are elderly or even visit folks on their deathbed. Ask them what mattered most in their life.

Philosophers have written extensively about the basic questions facing all human beings: Who am I? Where did I come from, and where will I go after I die? Does life have meaning? Am I ultimately alone?

How do we deal with such questions? Historically, people have relied on a range of philosophical, mythic, and religious narratives to provide answers in the face of fundamental uncertainty. More recently, we have turned to psychiatry and psychology and pharmacology for answers, or at least to feel better in the meantime. Sweat lodges, meditation, climbing mountain peaks, and trekking to the North Pole are among the means used by seekers.

But what really do we have to sustain us as life becomes more complex and losses mount as a natural consequence of living longer? Perhaps it is being tethered to at least one other person who is available at our beck and call; one person to whom we can reach out, whom we can touch, and by whom we can be touched in return. I submit to you that the most powerful sustenance available to us is another person who's interested and who cares. He or she serves as our go-to person, the one individual we can always count on to be there for us. Being available in this way is perhaps the most valuable gift you can give your partner.

In early childhood, our go-to person hopefully was our primary caregiver. In adulthood, the go-to person should be our primary partner. Unlike our early caregivers, our adult partner relies on the benefits of tethering in exactly the same way we do; that is, equally and mutually. In other words, while our early tethering was one-way, or asymmetric, our adult tethering should be symmetric.

If you are an anchor you already know all of this, so please bear with me. If you are an island or wave—especially what I've termed (in chapter 3) a wild island or wild wave—we have some chatting to do. The idea of tethering is problematic for you, isn't it? If you're an island, you probably don't believe much in tethering. After all, you are good by yourself, and others can be such a bother. If you're a wave, you believe in tethering, but it's a rather childish and one-way kind. You want to be tethered, but you either don't expect it in return or are unwilling to give it in return.

# WIRED FOR TETHERING

In addition to the role played by our early primary caregivers, the brain can set us up for easy tethering…or not. Helen Fisher, a social anthropologist and researcher on romantic love, and her colleagues (Fisher, Aron, and Brown 2005) report that during courtship, couples' brains are awash in excitatory neurotransmitters and hormones, such as noradrenaline and dopamine. Some of the same areas of the brain that are involved in addiction behaviors, such as the *ventral tegmental* area (where dopamine is produced), also are activated in romantic love. This accounts for the addictive qualities so characteristic of the infatuation phase of a relationship. Although noradrenaline and dopamine are plentiful in the infatuated brain, serotonin, a calming neurotransmitter, is in low supply. Hence the obsessive, anxious, and worried aspect of romantic love.

Couples who make it beyond the courtship phase and into a more secure, settled phase—notably anchors—have a more active *raphe nucleus*, where serotonin is produced. They are able to readily calm down and relax with one another. We could say they are wired to tether with one another. Island and wave partners, on the other hand, tend to have a less active raphe nucleus. These couples remain anxious and worried; they aren't able to tether properly, and do not easily and willingly serve as go-to people for each other.

# EXERCISE: YOUR CHILDHOOD GO-TO PEOPLE

Before you commit to being the go-to person for your partner, you may find it helpful to take a look at your own early experiences. Chances are that how you related to go-to people as a child will influence how you approach being the go-to person in your current relationship.

1. Ask yourself, to whom did I go as a child? And for what? Stop for a moment and think about the go-to people in your early life. Think back as far as you can remember. To whom did you run (or even crawl)? If it was a parent, which parent was it?

2. See if you can recall any specific incidents, however small they might have been. Perhaps you had a nightmare and called for your mother. Maybe she brought you a glass of warm milk. Or perhaps you got a boo-boo on the nursery school playground, and the teacher took you inside and put some ointment on it.

3. As you recall these incidents, see if you also can remember to what degree you felt safe with your go-to people. Could you count on them? Or were there times when your go-to people let you down? Perhaps a particular go-to person who repeatedly let you down? If so, were you able to find a new go-to person with whom you felt safer?

4. Finally, ask yourself what your relationship is today with the most important go-to people from your childhood. Are you still in close touch? Do you still go to them for anything?

# A MIND TO KNOW MINE

Childhood is not elective. Our earliest relationships are not chosen by us, and we do not get to decide how they function. We can't demand that they be fair, that they be just, that they be sensitive to our needs. We can't demand our earliest relationships include caregivers who want to know who we are and everything about us. In adulthood, however, our relationships are elective. At least that's the case for most of us in the Western world. We get to choose our partners and how our relationships will function. We can demand these relationships be fair, that they be just, and that our partners be sensitive to our needs. We can also expect that our partners will want to know who we are and everything about us. But here's the rub: do we actually *want* someone to know everything about us?

If you're an island, like Brian you're probably thinking, "Shouldn't some things be private?" In an insecure relationship, the automatic answer would be yes. It would make sense to keep to yourself anything that might cause trouble with your partner or jeopardize the sense of being able to do whatever you please, with whom you please, whenever you please. For example, although

Brian is 100 percent faithful to Marsha, he keeps from her certain details about his friendships with other women. He is afraid she doesn't trust him enough, and therefore he would have to give up those friendships—however harmless they might be—if she discovered how much he enjoyed them.

In a secure relationship, maintaining private compartments—whether having to do with money, sexuality, shameful events, or even any conceivable threat to one's partner—is counterproductive. Partners in a relationship based on mutuality agree they will feel safer and more secure if they fully know each other. Their goal is for both to be themselves within the relationship. Even if this is not possible in the outside world, they can be who they truly are with each other. They completely avail themselves to one another and grant permission to share whatever is on their mind, without reservation. In this sense, they have in each other *a mind to know mine*. And they agree to be go-to people for each other.

Islands and waves, on the other hand, often spread themselves among many different people. No one person knows everything about them (except perhaps in the case of a wave who chooses someone other than his or her primary partner as a confidante, and tells everything to that individual). Why do islands and waves do this? Because in their eyes, elevating someone to primary attachment status makes that person dangerous. At the slightest provocation by that partner, their amygdalae run wild. And of course they want to avoid this.

By contrast, let's look at a couple who have agreed to tell each other everything, no matter how difficult that may be, and regardless of whether it gets them into trouble.

## I WILL TELL YOU EVERYTHING

Eden and David have each taken the vow "I will tell you everything." Naturally, simply making this promise doesn't mean it will be easy, or guarantee either will do it at all times. But it does mean each will hold the other to the vow, because they both know it serves them well. And it means they will not tell anyone else something without first informing the partner. Neither will go to an individual therapist and tell him or her something about which the partner is not privy. Neither will go to his or her family of origin, or friends, or acquaintances, and reveal anything the partner doesn't already know.

"I had a weird experience today, and I'm afraid it makes me seem like a bad person," Eden says as she sits on the toilet with the door open, talking to David, who's combing his hair.

I know this may sound strange and even a bit disgusting, but in my experience as a couple therapist, I have found that partners who fear—how to do I say this delicately?—going to the bathroom in front of each other also fear telling each other everything. I haven't done any hard research on this; it's simply anecdotal evidence. Certainly, plenty of partners who don't tell each other everything have no such inhibitions. But the reverse seems true enough. I've also found this to be the case for partners who fear breathing on each other or anything else that feels too private. But let's return to our couple.

"Yeah? Tell me about it," David says with interest.

"I was in line at the market behind this old woman who was really unkempt. She smelled. I thought, 'How does a person get like that?' Really, it was repulsive. I almost shifted into another line to get away from her. But then she turned and gave me a warm smile as she put down one of those dividers to separate her food from mine. I felt really ashamed of myself. She was so sweet. And I had no clue. Has anything like that happened to you?"

"Nope," David replies flippantly. "But my day was uneventful. I just masturbated and waited for you to get home."

They both laugh.

"You are so weird," says Eden.

"Yeah, but I'm *your* weird," he says. "And don't you forget it."

"I love that we can say things like this to each other," says Eden.

On another occasion, after coming home from work, Eden informs David that a coworker came on to her at the office. She doesn't mention his name—not because she's withholding information, but because she knows it won't particularly matter to David.

In fact, he jumps straight to a different question. "What did you do about it?"

"I told him I'm happily married," Eden replies, giving David a kiss.

"How creepy," David continues. "Is he going to be a problem?"

"No," says Eden. "Don't worry. I can handle him."

Because this couple are accustomed to telling each other everything, they don't spend time entangled in jealousy or issues of trust. They are able to get straight to the point, which in this case is Eden's comfort level at work.

Rather than reacting out of threat, David is focused on confirming her safety and security.

## AUXILIARY BRAINS

One way to think of a *mind to know mine* is this: My partner and I represent two separate brains. Often, however, I can benefit from having an additional brain into which my thoughts can expand, a kind of auxiliary brain to help me to work things out. In this way, I can use my willing partner's brain as an extension of my own to find creative solutions to problems that might elude me if I were dependent on my own crowded brain.

This notion of expanding into another's mind is not new. For instance, Donald Winnicott (1957), a psychoanalyst, believed in the importance of providing a shared-mind space for his patients, a space he likened to the shared psychic space of infant and mother. This shared-mind space was valuable for therapy, and it's an important perk for partners who share a couple bubble.

Quite simply, two brains are better than one. Tethered partners can, in effect, lend and borrow their respective brains and nervous systems, thereby at least momentarily becoming more and having the capacity to accomplish more than either could with only one brain and nervous system. This also comes in handy when acting as competent managers of each other.

How might this look?

Take the example of Zane and Bobby, a thirty-something same-sex couple who tend to argue about Zane's smoking. One evening Zane comes home reeking of cigarettes.

"Did you smoke again?" Bobby asks.

"Yeah, I did," Zane replies sheepishly.

"Zane!" Bobby snaps.

"Yeah, I know I smell," says Zane.

"I thought you weren't going to do that anymore," says Bobby plaintively.

"No, I never said that. You said that; I didn't agree," argues Zane. "I said I would try not to do it around you and not lie about it when I did. On that we agreed."

"Yeah, yeah," Bobby mutters.

Though this may not sound like a good resolution, the fact that Zane didn't hesitate to admit what he had done is in keeping with their agreement to tell each other only the truth. It provides a basis from which they can work together, in a shared-mind space, toward Zane's smoking cessation—if that is in fact what he really wants.

Or take a different example.

Charlotte and Toby, a couple in their late fifties, find themselves with increasing responsibilities for two sets of aging parents. Late one night, after they have gone to bed, Helen receives a phone call from her father, who explains that her mother fell in the bathroom and is now on her way to the emergency room with a suspected broken hip.

Charlotte gets dressed, then wakes Toby. "Mom needs me," she says, and explains she is driving to the hospital.

She kisses him goodbye, but Toby is swinging his feet to the side of the bed. "I'm coming with you."

"Really?" she says. "I thought you have an early meeting."

"Don't worry, I'll call in if it looks like I might be late," he says. "You'll have your hands full with your dad at the hospital, especially if your mom needs surgery."

"Oh," says Charlotte. "Dad's still at home."

"At home?" Toby echoes, shooting her a look that says, "What are you thinking?"

"Mom went in the ambulance," she explains. "It was too much for Dad to manage with his walker."

"So that's what I'll do," says Toby, pulling on his jacket.

"What?" asks Charlotte. "You mean go there?"

"I'll take the spare key and let myself in. If he's sleeping, I won't disturb him. But if he's up—or when he gets up—I'll make sure he takes his meds and has something to eat. Then I'll bring him to the hospital."

"Yes," says Charlotte, quickly getting onboard with the plan. "That would be so helpful. And if there are any new developments with Mom, I'll text you right away."

"I'll be napping on the sofa if your dad's asleep."

Charlotte fishes in her purse and hands Toby the spare key to her parent's house. "What would I do without you?" she says, shaking her head. "I was assuming Dad would have to fend for himself until I could get over there. This is so much better."

---

## EXERCISE: SPILLING THE BEANS

This one is for those of you who don't like to be asked, "What are you thinking?" You probably respond with something like "Nothing." The problem is, unless you are brain dead, there's always something on your mind. So, if you're game, try this little exercise.

1. Agree that you and your partner will ask, when the other is least expecting it, "What are you thinking?"

2. The other must answer without hesitation. "Nothing" won't cut it. And don't worry about significance. If you're thinking about tying your shoe, say that. If you're thinking about burnt toast, say that.

3. Practice until both of you can respond without thinking about what to say.

So why do this? Because having an open mind with your partner means it isn't up to you to decide what's relevant to share. If you are used to spilling the beans with little things, it will be easier to communicate openly when something big comes along.

---

# THE 24/7 AGREEMENT

As we discussed in Chapter 1, partners who create a couple bubble enter into an agreement to put the relationship before anything and everything else. They agree to abide by the principle "We come first." One of the specific agreements they can make to carry this out is to serve as the go-to person for one another. A related agreement is that each will be available to the other 24 hours a day, 7 days a week.

When I say 24/7, I mean it literally. Each partner must enjoy a 24/7 hotline to the other. In other words, if one partner wants to call the other in the middle of the day simply to report an itch on the nose, his or her partner is expected to answer cheerfully—as in "It's great to hear from you!" This privilege can be enjoyed by both partners at any time. So, for example, if you are my partner, and we're in bed, and I can't sleep because I'm anxious about the day, I can wake you up, and you will be there to help me without any feeling of resentment. Why? Because I must do the very same for you, if not in that situation, then in other circumstances when it likely will be inconvenient for me. That is our agreement. It is our assurance to one another that we aren't alone, that we have a tether to one another. We do this for each other because we want to. We do it because we can. And because we appreciate how loved and secure it makes us feel. We wouldn't ask it of anyone else, and nobody else would want to do it for us.

Now, does this mean everybody should expect to be able to instantly contact his or her partner each and every time? Of course not. If you have that itch on your nose and your partner is high over the Atlantic on a business trip, you're unlikely to phone the airline. However, the point is that couples should feel secure in knowing they can reach out to their partner at any time, anywhere, and their partner will be receptive. Moreover, this availability works both ways.

## It's Okay to Be High Maintenance

Partners in a couple bubble who agree to be available go-to people for each other benefit in ways nobody outside the bubble can. To be sure, maintenance of this agreement can feel burdensome at times, but the effort is well worth the trouble. Partners who expect one another to be available 24/7 are and should be considered high maintenance.

In our culture, being labeled high maintenance usually is considered a pejorative. Typically, men speak about a woman as high maintenance if they see her as demanding attention, overly concerned about her appearance, or hard to please. This is not what I mean here. I am speaking about two people who are willing to go the extra mile for each other. They are willing to put in the highest level of effort possible, for their mutual benefit. They are willing to give freely, knowing they will receive the same in return. They are high maintenance because they expect their partner to be at their beck and call. If I seem to be belaboring the point, it is only because I'm aware that what I'm describing runs counter to some of our basic assumptions about how relationships should function.

# EXERCISE: MAP YOUR GO-TO NETWORK

So you and your partner have agreed to be each other's go-to people. How is this working out for you? Use this exercise to find out more about how you actually use each other as go-to people. You can do this exercise either on your own or as a couple.

1. Throughout the week, make a note each time one of you "goes to" the other. Jot down the reason for doing so. It can be something consequential for your relationship or something that just feels important in the moment. For example, it might be to complain about the loud music your neighbor's teenager is playing, and to decide who should speak to his parents. Or it might be to get a backrub for sore and tense shoulders. Or to share a crimson sunset visible from the kitchen window. My list would include the many times throughout the day that my wife and I go to each other to share momentary, sometimes silly, experiences.

2. Of course, even if you have agreed to be each other's primary go-to people, you will both go to various others throughout the week. Make note of your interactions with some of these secondary go-to people, as well, and your reasons for going to them. If you're doing this on your own, you may have limited information about your partner's secondary go-to people.

3. You may choose to record (or summarize) your go-to data in a chart that illustrates your go-to network.

    If you and your partner are doing this exercise together, you can each take a separate piece of paper and start by drawing a big circle in the center to represent yourself. Now place your partner in relation to you. Are you both in the circle? Add others to whom you go for help, gossiping, hanging out, or whatever. Where are these people in relation to yourself and your partner? Are any in competition with your partner? Compare your charts and see if you appear to be the primary go-to people for each other. If not, talk about it and redraw your chart so your placement as the first to know everything is clarified.

4. At the end of the week, sit down and review your experience—either by yourself or with your partner. Did you and your partner actually go to each other as often as you thought you might? Were there times one of you wanted to go to the other, but didn't? If so, why didn't you?

Do you notice anything about your secondary go-to people that you might want to change? For example, when one couple compiled their chart, she discovered he had gone to his mother about organizing his dad's birthday party several days before he mentioned it to his partner. He apologized for this oversight and promised to keep her more informed about his side of the family in the future. He then pointed out with a smile that he could have fixed the stuck drain himself if she had asked him before she called in the handyman.

# SIXTH GUIDING PRINCIPLE

The sixth principle in this book is that *partners should serve as the primary go-to people for one another*. I have observed that partners who create and maintain a tether to one another experience more personal safety and security, have more energy, take more risks, and experience overall less stress than couples who do not. When you commit to serving as a go-to person for your partner, you open the door for your partner to do the same for you. Then you both can enjoy free and unencumbered access to one another in terms of time and of mind. In this way, you build synergy in your relationship, such that you are able to operate together in ways that are greater than if you each lived as essentially separate individuals.

If you recall, this notion of "two can be better than one" was our descriptor of an anchor in Chapter 3. Our sample anchor couple, Mary and Pierce, acted as go-to people for each other and explicitly stated that they could tell each other everything. Similarly, by agreeing to become go-to people for each other, you and your partner can take a giant step toward ensuring that you become anchors for one another.

Here are some supporting principles to guide you:

1. Make a formal agreement to be available to each other 24/7. Couples often find that formally stating their agreement gives it added oomph. It is easier to hold to an agreement later, in the heat of the moment, when it has been explicitly made and both of you have bought in.

   This also gives you a chance to voice any resistance, hesitations, · or trepidations. If one of you is an island or wave, you might discuss how you feel about being tethered to your partner. Look both at what scares you and at how you stand to benefit from maintaining this tether. Brainstorm ways to handle any situations in which you might be tempted to withhold yourself.

   It can be mutually reinforcing to verbalize your agreement regularly. Remember the Emote Me Game? Saying "I'm always here for you, darling" or "You can talk to me about anything, anytime" or "I'm all yours, 24/7" can move your partner.

2. Develop go-to signals with your partner. Especially initially, you and your partner may find it helpful to have ways to let each other know you are in need of contact. If your partner is an island, for instance, he or she may appreciate a signal that helps ease into being fully available. You might say, "Excuse me, I realize you're in the middle of XYZ, but I need a few minutes to talk about…"

   Signals don't have to be verbal. You can give a certain look or make a certain gesture to communicate to your partner that he or she has your full attention. For example, taking both your partner's hands in yours might be an indication that everything else needs to be dropped so you can focus on each other and the needs of the moment.

3. Recognize your need to be tethered. At first blush, the idea of relying on one person may seem too threatening. You may think that the more people you can rally to your support, the more secure you'll feel. After all, compared with relating to your partner, relating to others is a piece of cake, right?

   It may seem that way. But don't be fooled. Yes, of course, no other relationship comes with the same burdens of expectation, dependency, and needfulness you experience with your primary partner. But herein lies the saving grace. The expectations you and your partner have of each other may be higher, but so are the potential rewards.

Often, I think, we don't take the time to get clear about our expectations of one another. We don't get specific about what we need from our partner. Yes, you want him or her to make you feel safe and secure, loved and cared for. But how? What do you actually want and need from your primary go-to person?

This is a question I can't and wouldn't want to answer for you. You must do that yourself, or with your partner, for the answer to be meaningful. However, I can report what I have observed among happily tethered couples. These partners are there for each other's deep emotional needs. This means being able to share and discuss all their feelings, worries, concerns, and doubts, as well as all the joys and emotional highs. It means sharing old secrets and memories. It means revealing crushes and infatuations and fantasies. At the same time, these partners are available 24/7 for things that to anyone else outside the relationship might seem trivial or not worth a moment's time: anything from the way your toenail is growing in, to the sound the ice maker in your refrigerator makes, to the latest joke someone sent you in an e-mail.

# CHAPTER 7

# Protecting the Couple Bubble: How to Include Outsiders

W e humans may appear at times to be animals that run in packs, but we are basically creatures who form twosomes. We start as a twosome with our birth mother and branch out to other twosomes. If another adult, such as a father, competes for our mother's attention, we learn at a young age to move over and accept being squeezed out of their exclusive relationship from time to time. It's a bummer at the time, yes. But it also prepares us for threesomes, foursomes, and more to come. We learn how to be a third wheel around our parents, and this ability to take a backseat allows us to form other twosomes, while understanding the value of and need for exclusivity.

This matter of twosomes and threesomes is a very important aspect of the owner's manual to your relationship. As we've discussed, our security is dependent upon our ability to become tethered to one person. We choose one person with whom to form an adult partnership, much as young children know to whom they can run when scared or in pain or excited. Through this adult twosome, we look to one person above all others for comfort and immediate care.

Yet we as couples are not alone in the world. We may be two, but there is always a third to be found somewhere. By a *third* I mean third people, third objects, third tasks, or anything else that could intrude on a couple bubble or make it difficult to form one. For example, third people can include children, in-laws, other extended family members, friends, business partners and bosses, and even strangers. Third things can be work, hobbies, video games, TV shows . . . and the list can go on and on. On occasion, thirds can be easily incorporated into a couple bubble. For example, if you and your partner both enjoy bird watching, you will naturally bring this hobby into your life together. But if you like bird watching while your partner prefers football, it is likely to be more challenging to bring your respective thirds into the relationship.

In this chapter, we focus on how couples handle thirds. Specifically, we look at how couples handle four of the most important types of thirds: in-laws, children, drugs and alcohol, and affairs.

# THE THREAT OF THE THIRD

Couples who handle thirds poorly typically do so before they even enter into their relationship. A good couple therapist can spot this pattern immediately by noticing how partners talk about other people, and most strikingly, how they talk about each other in front of the therapist. These folks constantly marginalize their primary partner. They betray one another by forming exclusive and excluding pairings with other people and things. For example, one partner might take his sister's side over his partner's side, while the other partner is more wedded to her wine than to her spouse. Both form unholy alliances with their children. Neither serves as the go-to person for the other, or is dedicated to the other's safety and security. They are either unable to form or unable to maintain a true couple bubble.

To be sure, these are not bad people. In fact, they are normal, everyday people who simply have never developed productive ways of relating to outsiders—people and things outside their twosome. They aren't wired for secure love. These partners may be either islands or waves, or they may simply be young and inexperienced. Perhaps their own parents at times broke their couple bubble and inappropriately let their children in, setting the stage for later confusion.

## OVERACTIVE PRIMITIVES, UNDERACTIVE AMBASSADORS

Having overactive primitives and/or underactive ambassadors can make it difficult for couples to include outsiders in their relationship. If an island's primitives are constantly sounding the alarm, for instance, her or she may opt to focus on an object or task. To the primitives, time spent with this third—be it work, or a hobby, or an addiction—is safer and more relaxing than time with a partner.

Very young children engage in this kind of isolated behavior. Psychologists call it *parallel play*, and it is most typical among children aged two or three. Several children play together in the same room, each with their own toy, but without engaging each other. As children age and their ambassadors mature, they become adept at playing together. Two children learn to play amicably with the same toy. Later they're able to include additional playmates—thirds—as well. If adult couples depend on what is essentially parallel play, we can deduce that their ambassadors are being railroaded by their primitives.

Waves also can fall under the sway of their primitives. They are less likely than islands to engage in parallel play, and more likely to seek out other people as thirds. Their primitives may drive them to do this as a means of punishing a partner whom they perceive as unavailable or rejecting. Instead of bringing a third person into their relationship in a nonthreatening manner, they shuttle between the third and their partner. This tug-of-war leads to endless friction and strife, typically sending the ambassadors further into hiding.

Partners who don't know how to bring thirds into their twosome find themselves continually destabilized by others who come along. Often they run into particular trouble when they have children. To their chagrin, either parent, and sometimes both, can be dethroned at a moment's notice. They feel left out, lonely, insecure, or threatened. Many fights and breakups center on the failure to properly include thirds, without either partner recognizing this is the problem. Usually, the partner feeling betrayed focuses on the third person or thing he or she perceives as a threat, without stopping to notice how he or she may be threatening the relationship in the same manner. The inability of partners to effectively include outsiders in their duo almost always is reciprocal in nature.

Many of the couples featured in this book do a poor job of handling threatening thirds. See if you can go through the chapters you've already read and find which ones.

---

## EXERCISE: WHO ARE YOUR THIRDS?

In the last chapter, you mapped your network of go-to people. Possibly some of your or your partner's secondary go-to people function as thirds in your relationship. I suggest you take a fresh look now and identify the people who most often make your relationship a threesome.

Who might they be?

1. Other family members, such as children and parents, make natural thirds. You may not think of them as outsiders because you're all in the same family, but they are outsiders with respect to your twosome.

2. Other common thirds are friends with whom you engage socially. When you and your partner socialize with another couple, they count as a third together.

3. And don't forget thirds that aren't people. What activities do you and your partner do that function as thirds in your relationship?

As you make a list of your thirds, notice which are included effectively within your relationship. How do you feel in the presence of these thirds? What makes for smooth relating with them from the vantage point of your couple bubble?

---

# IN-LAWS AS THIRDS

For most couples, in-laws come with the relationship. Initially, these are parents-in-law and siblings-in-law, but later on they may include daughters-in-law and sons-in-law. The examples I've provided here are of the former type; however, the principle is the same for both.

## LETTING THE WRONG ONE IN

Suzanne and Klaus, both in their thirties, have two young children. Suzanne is very close to her father, now widowed. In the first years of marriage, Klaus admired his father-in-law and sought out his company. They had long discussions about politics, a subject of interest to both. However, this relationship soured when Klaus and Suzanne's second child was a toddler, and Suzanne started calling on her father for babysitting help so she could go back to work part time at the job she'd quit before the child's birth. Soon the couple found themselves continually interacting with and about a third wheel in their relationship.

In fact, the problem here isn't actually the third wheel. It isn't Suzanne's father himself. To be very clear about this: thirds—whether people or things— usually start off as neutral to all parties. If they become negative, it's generally because one partner marginalizes the other, making him or her take on the role of third wheel in some way. There are exceptions, to be sure, such as nasty habits, addictions, and affiliations with horrible people, that start off and remain bad to the sidelined partner. But understand that most outside people and things become positive or negative depending on how partners relate to that third. If one partner's position in the couple bubble is demoted or downgraded as a result of the third's intrusion, you can be sure that third person or thing will become hated.

When Klaus realized Suzanne was sharing private matters with her father that she did not share first with him, he became angry and upset. They argued frequently, and Klaus grew increasingly hostile toward his father-in-law's role in their family.

Their conversations sounded something like this:

"I don't want him coming over tonight," Klaus says when Suzanne announces she has invited her father for dinner. "In fact, I don't really want him here at all anymore."

"He's my dad," she asserts. "Plus he's done a lot for this family. If it weren't for him, I wouldn't be able to work, which is something you support. Remember? Besides, what horrible thing has he ever done to you?"

"I've told you," Klaus growls. "He disapproves of everything I do. Especially anything involving you."

Suzanne crosses her arms, preparing for the fight she knows is coming. "Daddy likes you, but of course he loves me." She pauses. "You have to admit, I haven't been happy the last six months."

Klaus bristles. "You mean happy with *me*?"

"With you, yes."

"So you're unhappy *because* of *me?*" he repeats.

"I'd be happier if you'd be more of a father to your children."

Klaus glares at his wife. "My relationship with the kids is just fine, thank you."

"Then why do they always want grandpa?" she counters. "They run to him for hugs—"

"I can't believe you're comparing me with your dad, saying he's a better father than I am!"

"Just saying."

"Like he was a stellar father to you, right?" Klaus rages. "Everything you told me about him never being around, being abusive to your mom and you, drinking too much—you call that good fathering? I've never screamed at the kids."

"But you're not around a lot of the time, are you? Work comes before family with you."

Klaus's voice drops. "You know, I don't feel much like your husband right now. It kills me that you'd rather have your dad here than me."

Suzanne frowns. "No, I want you here. You know that. I just want you to be civil to my dad. If you can't do it for him, can you at least do it for me and the kids?"

"Does that work both ways?" Klaus demands. "What will you do when he starts criticizing me in front of our kids? Or wants to tell me how to relate to my own family? What then?"

Suzanne stands up, signaling an end to the conversation. "You want to be the man of the house, you deal with him. And don't threaten me," she says, heading off to prepare dinner.

As you can see, Suzanne is furious with Klaus. She resents his focus on work, which in her mind leaves him free from the burdens of household chores and child rearing. Although her father was a poor parent, he has redeemed himself and become the father she always wanted. Instead of finding an effective way to include her father in her relationship with Klaus, she has let her father in while chasing Klaus out. Ultimately, because of Suzanne's poor handling of thirds, Klaus despises her father and resents his own children. At the same time, Klaus's poor handling of thirds has led Suzanne to despise both his work and his colleagues.

# LETTING THE RIGHT ONE IN

Perry and Landa, another couple in their thirties with two children, regularly have family over for dinner. This week, Perry's family is coming for Friday night supper. The guests include Perry's mother and father, and his sister, her husband, and their young child. Perry's mother and sister have had a rocky history with Landa since before the couple's wedding. Neither Landa nor Perry approves of the sister's parenting style, and both dread spending time with her when the child is present.

However, over the past few years, Perry and Landa have worked out a strategy for dealing with family get-togethers. They have learned to plan ahead and discuss what might be difficult, and what they'll do if that problem arises. They agree to stick together as a team, protecting their couple bubble and maintaining an "us and them" stance. They make escape plans if either needs to leave the room or end the evening earlier than expected. They agree to make frequent eye contact as a means of checking in, to look at each other while they include others in their conversations, and to devise other cues to communicate with one another without making their guests uncomfortable. Neither is afraid to use a well-timed whisper to communicate a private message without appearing rude.

It's show time as Perry's mother and father arrive early. The children greet their grandparents with glee, then retreat into their rooms. As her mother-in-law joins Landa in the kitchen, Perry checks Landa's eyes for signs that she is alright and he isn't needed. Perry takes his father into the living room, where they drink and talk business. Moments later his sister arrives with her husband and son. Again, the children greet everyone and invite their cousin into their room. The sister joins Landa and her mother-in-law in the kitchen, and her husband joins the men in the living room. Again, Landa and Perry use eye contact to check for signs of distress. Aside from an eye-widening glance with which Landa conveys that this isn't her favorite social situation, she gives him the all clear sign.

After several moments, Perry hears his mother's voice become louder and her tone shriller. He gets up and checks on Landa in the kitchen. This time she gives a more sustained cue that she is tiring of both women. He goes up to her, makes her stop what she's doing, throws his arms around her, and says

125

to her quietly how lucky he is to have her. He can feel her relax in his arms. She kisses him, and he starts to engage the other two women.

"How about we go into the living room? We can all talk together there," he says, ushering his mother and sister out and leaving Landa to finish dinner preparations.

On the sofa, Perry finds himself flanked by his mother and sister, with his father catty-corner on the loveseat and his brother-in-law standing by the fireplace. When Landa enters, cocktail in hand, she notices this arrangement. Perry immediately gets up and asks his father to move to the sofa so he and Landa can have the loveseat. Landa and Perry's strategy for maintaining their couple bubble is to control where they sit, especially in situations where others use seating to split them up. They do the same at the dinner table so they can use one another for comfort and support.

While Perry is sensitive to Landa's need for comfort and support, she is equally aware of his need for the same. Perry's sister often gets the better of him, and Landa helps minimize the stress he feels when conversing with his sister. She knows the cues that signal Perry's distress, such as a tendency to talk too fast and increased complaints about tension in his neck.

When the get-together is over, Perry and Landa congratulate one another for a job well done, as they gossip through kitchen clean-up. They are pleased with their ability to host dinners with their in-laws without causing fights between the two of them, and without causing distress to their guests. Because they do this so smoothly, neither ever feels like a third wheel.

# CHILDREN AS THIRDS

Often couples who poorly manage thirds of one type do just as poorly with thirds of another type. How to include their children in their relationship is a particularly critical question for couples.

## OUT IN THE COLD

Suzanne and Klaus's children are Brian, age nine, and Tammy, age six. Now that both children are in school, Suzanne is able to work part time without the need to frequently call on her father for babysitting. Because of Klaus's work schedule, he is less involved with the child care than she is.

Typically, Klaus arrives home late and wants to see the kids before doing anything else. He feels he spends too little time with them as it is, and wants to be playful whenever possible. This irritates Suzanne, who not only wants the kids to wind down at night, but resents that she doesn't get the same greeting and attention from them as Klaus does when he comes home. This latter complaint she keeps to herself.

Klaus plays with both Tammy and Brian, then retreats to his and Suzanne's bedroom to do some last minute work on his laptop, leaving her to deal with the now hyped-up kids. One night, his laptop comfortably on his lap as he stretches out on the bed, Klaus hears sharp vocal tones interrupting the lilting music coming through his earbuds. As the voices become disturbingly shrill, he realizes Suzanna is arguing with Tammy. Reluctantly leaving the bed, he tracks the voices down the stairs and into the living room.

"Turn off that TV!" Suzanne is yelling, mustering all the authority she can. "I gave you a five-minute warning, and you just ignored it. The TV goes off *now*!"

"Why?" Tammy wails. "Daddy, tell her to stop!"

"What's going on?" Klaus asks Suzanne.

"I told her five minutes, and the TV had be off so she can get ready for bed. I'm tired of this same battle every night! It's already past bedtime."

"I'm not tired!" Tammy screams. "And she didn't say five minutes."

"She didn't," Brian chimes in. "Tammy's right."

"It's not fair!" Tammy's voice continues to escalate as she makes her case to Klaus.

"Maybe they didn't hear the warning," Klaus says calmly to Suzanne.

Suzanne's eyes widen and her nostrils flare. "What?" she says in disbelief.

"'Maybe they didn't hear you' is all I said." Klaus looks with disdain as Suzanne gestures wildly. "Hey, calm down."

"Okay, you handle it!" Suzanne snaps. "You put them to bed tonight!"

Klaus watches helplessly as his wife grabs her purse and car keys and flies out the door. In that instant, she might be the one leaving, but both partners feel they've lost the battle. Each has left the other out in the cold. At a time when they should be a unified parenting force in the eyes of their children—the thirds in their relationship—it's their children who are calling the shots, pitting the parents against each other, making both Mom and Dad into third wheels.

Trying to calm himself, Klaus sits down on the sofa. Apparently accustomed to sudden departures by their mother, Tammy and Brian climb onto his lap and watch another fifteen minutes of television.

## WARMLY INCLUDED

Perry and Landa's two kids are Jamie, age ten, and Sara, age eight. When Perry comes home for dinner, he and Landa have agreed, they will reunite before he greets the children. To accomplish this, he often phones just prior to arriving. Landa then knows to greet him near or at the door. They embrace until fully relaxed, make and sustain eye contact long enough to refocus attention on one another, and check that each feels adjusted to the home environment. Only then do they turn their attention to the children and other activities.

Later in the evening, while Perry is helping Sara prepare for bed, he hears Landa struggling with Jamie downstairs. Jamie is angry about losing his computer game privileges because he didn't finish his homework. Though Landa is more than capable of handling Jamie's opposition, tonight she is low on resources. Perry senses from the tone of her voice that her patience is reaching a breaking point.

Perry gives Sara a quick squeeze and promises to be back in a jiffy, then rushes downstairs. He walks into the room, stands beside Landa so she can feel their solidarity, and kisses her on the cheek. Then he says with good humor, "Let's kill him."

All three laugh at the absurd suggestion, which serves as an instant adjustment toward calm for each of them.

Sensing his parent's solidarity, Jamie heaves a sigh and picks up his math book.

Perry again kisses Landa's cheek, whispers, "Good job," and leaves the room. He quickly returns to Sara.

Landa and Perry maintain their couple bubble by handling thirds properly. Just as they are able to relate to their in-laws without leaving anyone out in the cold, they're able to include both children. At no time does either partner make the other a third wheel, demote or devalue the other's position of authority, or forget to provide soothing and support. Their children pick up on this and feel warmly included.

# DRUGS AND ALCOHOL AS THIRDS

Many couples treat their addictions or compulsive behaviors as thirds. Most commonly, these addictions are drugs and/or alcohol. Others include sex and pornography, flirting, gambling, food, online social networking, shopping and spending, obsessive cleaning or hoarding, a compulsive need for alone time, a compulsive need to socialize, and many more.

## BEHIND MY BACK

Klaus comes from a family of alcohol users. To some extent, this reflects his German heritage, which sanctions a high level of beer and wine consumption. However, according to Klaus, his father went beyond the norm for his culture and is a card-carrying alcoholic to this day. Suzanne complains that Klaus is headed down the same track. She accuses him of sneaking drinks, and she's worried that if he doesn't cut back now, their children will be exposed to his inappropriate behavior. This is a source of increasingly frequent fights between them.

"Don't think I don't know when you've had a drink," she says. "You become a different person when you drink."

"What do you mean?" says Klaus. "How?"

"You become silly and sloppy. You're not my Klaus anymore."

"I thought you like me when I get silly. You say I'm funny and fun to be with," Klaus replies in his defense.

"It's true that when we're out with friends, you can be funny," Suzanne admits. "But sometimes I feel embarrassed for you. You say things that make you look, I don't know, inebriated and foolish. Plus, you say private things about me that embarrass me. I hate it when you do that!" says Suzanne, becoming angrier as she recalls a recent incident.

"When have I ever said anything private?" Klaus responds, his voice growing louder.

Suzanne covers her mouth with her hand, and her eyes glaze over. She stands there deep in thought, as if running a disturbing movie in her mind.

Moments pass in silence. "I'm asking you," Klaus repeats, "when have I ever given private information in public?"

Suzanne shakes her head. "I don't want to tell you," she says mournfully. "You'll deny it because you won't remember."

"Try me."

"We were out with your business partner and his wife."

"At that new Italian restaurant," he adds.

"Right. And you'd had a few drinks. We started talking about getting enough sleep, and you told them I take a sleeping pill every night—"

"So? What's wrong with that?" Klaus interrupts.

"Wait!" Suzanne responds sharply, her hand flying up. "You didn't let me finish. You said I take a pill every night, which is none of their business. And then you went into detail about what I'm like afterward. You said I raid the refrigerator and don't remember it in the morning. That was humiliating. They didn't need to know that."

"I don't remember saying anything like that," Klaus responds defensively.

"I know you don't remember," says Suzanne. "That's what I said a minute ago. That's what makes it so humiliating. There I was, with this sloppy, obnoxious drunk who didn't even care what I was feeling. And with *your* friends!" Suzanne begins to tear up.

"That's mighty nervy coming from you, who takes sleeping pills and doesn't remember the next morning that we had sex," Klaus states angrily.

"That's different," says Suzanne, choking back tears. "I don't embarrass you in public."

"No," replies Klaus, "you say you don't need those pills. But then I see how you slur your speech and act stupid. One of these days I'm afraid you won't have the sense to wait till I'm home to medicate yourself, and the kids will see the mess you're in. I even had to hide your keys to stop you from driving to the store last week. Remember that? How do you think all this makes *me* feel? Not only am I with a drunk every night, but you're not with *me*."

After a long silence Suzanne speaks up. "I guess we both let something come between us—for me it's taking sleeping pills, and for you it's drinking."

"Yeah, I guess we do," sighs Klaus.

## I HAVE YOUR BACK

Landa and Perry both like to drink. Neither sees alcohol as a threat to their relationship. Rather, they view drinking as a source of shared enjoyment. They occasionally even smoke pot when friends are over and the kids are in bed asleep. However, if either becomes uncomfortable with this practice, the other respects his or her wishes and refrains.

When out to dinner with friends, each drinks wine. They agree ahead of time to monitor one another's drinking, because they know it's difficult to self-monitor. If one or the other notices a shift in behavior that could be attributed to the effects of the wine—or to anything else, for that matter—he or she will whisper into the other's ear, "That's enough." And that is taken as the cue to stop drinking.

If one or the other begins to launch into a potentially dangerous conversation with others, a squeeze on the leg gets the message across to "proceed with caution."

Both Landa and Perry appreciate this special service each provides for the other. Not only does it keep them safe and secure in their couple bubble, it keeps them safe with other people, as well. Both view themselves as the protector and regulator of the other in public, and each has saved the other in social situations where something easily could have been said or done that would have damaged an important relationship.

They have one another's backs.

---

## EXERCISE: GET YOUR SIGNALS STRAIGHT

As we've seen, Landa and Perry have a system of signals they use with each other in the company of thirds. You can do the same.

1. Take an inventory of your signals. Chances are you already use signals with your partner, even if you aren't consciously aware of it. The next time

you are with an outsider, notice the nonverbal ways you and your partner communicate. Notice, too, how quickly and accurately you pick up each other's signals.

2. Develop new signals. Having a private language of your own can be very effective, as well as fun. Children do this, and love it when you can't understand their secret code. Discuss with your partner how you might communicate in tricky situations with thirds, such as in the presence of in-laws or out in public. What, specifically, are the messages you need to give one another in these situations?

Keep in mind that your signals must be subtle and must be suited to your partner's sensitivities. It would be self-defeating, for instance, if your partner perceived your signal as a threat instead of the friendly assist you intended it to be. It also would be ill advised to adopt a loud signal that, say, led your son-in-law to feel your not-so-secret language was intended to exclude him.

3. Practice your new signals the next time a situation arises, and see how effective they are. Make sure you have your signals in order ahead of time!

# AFFAIRS AS THIRDS

Romantic and sexual affairs constitute perhaps the most obvious form thirds can take in a relationship. In my experience, infidelity is among the chief reasons couples seek therapy. The good news is that understanding how to protect their couple bubble can help couples save their relationship, even if one or both partners have undermined it by engaging in infidelity.

You might be wondering, how common is infidelity? That's hard to say. It depends on what statistics you read, and on how you define infidelity. The traditional definition focuses on extramarital sexual relations, whether as a one-night stand or a long-term involvement. Using this definition, a 2006 study of 10,000 adults conducted by Tom Smith from the University of Chicago's National Opinion Research Center reported that 22 percent of married men and 15 percent of married women had committed adultery at ·

least once. But many people define affairs more broadly. A survey (Weaver 2007) in which more than 70,000 adults estimated 44 percent of men and 36 percent of women had cheated lends support to the notion of a broader definition.

I'd like you to consider fidelity in terms of what it means to your couple bubble. Because both your and your partner's safety and security—your very survival—depend on mutual conservatorship, you can view fidelity as synonymous with couple bubble. Sexual infidelity is an obvious breach of fidelity. But so, for example, are the following:

♥ Emotional closeness with a third that leaves you or your partner out in the cold

♥ Sharing of one partner's secrets with a third

♥ Flirting online or sexting with a third

♥ Office romances or over-the-top flirting

♥ Use of pornography that excludes the other partner

# 2 + 1 = ZERO

You know the expression "Two is company, three is a crowd"? For couples who don't know how to include outsiders, three isn't just a crowd, it's a complete zero. By that, I mean their failure to form safe threesomes (or moresomes) can end up destroying what they have as a twosome. Let's go back to Klaus and Suzanne one more time.

Infidelity has been a continual threat to their relationship. Early on, Klaus had an intense but brief affair with someone from his office. The involvement ended after Suzanne discovered incriminating e-mails and gave Klaus an ultimatum. He assured her it never would have turned into anything serious, and she shouldn't feel threatened. However, ten years later, it is still in Suzanne's mind.

When Klaus has stayed extra late at the office or the couple has an argument or Suzanne is feeling insecure for no particular reason, their conversations go like this:

"How was your luncheon?" Suzanne asks the following morning, a Saturday, as they sit at the kitchen table over coffee.

"Oh, okay," says Klaus with a shrug. "You know, the usual pasta and salad. They even had a good dessert. Chocolate—"

"So, you sat next to Crystal?" Suzanne interrupts.

"Crystal?" Klaus scrunches up his face. "Yeah. So what?"

"How come you didn't say so? You think you can just talk about the food, and I'll ignore—"

This time Klaus cuts in. "What's there to say? I sat next to Crystal. Dave was on my other side. Relax! How many times do I have to tell you: absolutely nothing is going on between Crystal and me."

Suzanne isn't persuaded. "So you say. But I've seen how she looks at you. At the office Christmas party, you spent more time talking with her than you did with me. How am I supposed to relax when you continually give me cause to feel otherwise?"

"Jiminy! How many times must I explain?" Klaus's irritation is mounting; nothing he says to defend himself seems to budge Suzanne. "We were talking about a report due January 1st, and there was no time to work on it over the holidays. The truth is, it ruined the party for me. But I've already apologized for that. The question is, when will you let it go?"

Suzanne stops to consider this. In fact, she yearns to let go of her insecurities. It's just that she doesn't know how. Tears come to her eyes as she flashes back to Klaus's affair ten years before. "Maybe when you aren't always comparing me with other women," she says after a few moments.

Klaus is touched by her honesty. He wants to reach out, hold her close, and assure her that he loves her. At the same time, he feels a strong pang of guilt. Much as he loves Suzanne, he is frequently attracted to other women. He tells himself it's just one of those natural male-female things. Crystal, for example, is a smart, stylish professional, and he enjoys working with her. He likes lingering an extra moment as the target of her gorgeous smile. After all, he thinks, this kind of flirtation is harmless.

Klaus pauses. Why feel guilt over something so harmless? It occurs to him that confessing to Suzanne that he is sometimes attracted to other women might lessen his guilt.

But then he worries about what he might have to give up. Maybe he'll lose Crystal's friendship altogether. He feels ashamed at how much he is looking forward to seeing her Monday morning. Suddenly, instead of a confession, he blurts out, "For crying out loud, I'm not always comparing you with other women! Stop being paranoid. Do you have any idea how unattractive that is?"

You have probably recognized Klaus and Suzanne as waves. Both are ambivalent about connecting. They use thirds, in the form of affairs, to fuel their ambivalence. For Klaus, this means leaving his options open so he can buffer any potential dangers at home through connection with a third. For Suzanne, it means living with so much fear about an affair—whether real or imagined—that she can't fully commit to her marriage.

Islands have affairs for slightly different reasons. For them, the third tends to offer an escape valve in the relationship. An affair is viewed as an assertion of independence. Some islands make a philosophical or psychological argument in favor of polyamory (multiple love partners). They may encourage their partner to do likewise, and contend that jealousy is a non-issue for all parties involved. The legitimacy of this perspective is not for us to argue over here. Suffice to say, when it comes to protecting the couple bubble, any affair will be a deal breaker.

# 2 + 1 = NO PROBLEM

Affairs are not limited to islands and waves. Anchors have affairs, too. During the first year of her relationship with Perry, while they were dating steadily but not living together, Landa went for dinner with an old boyfriend from high school. She told Perry about it ahead of time and invited him to come along. However, trusting Landa and thinking she and her ex, whom she hadn't seen in years, might enjoy the time together, Perry declined.

Landa and her old boyfriend had a few drinks, and after he gave her a quick kiss good night, they ended up making out in his car.

First thing the next morning, Landa called Perry. She said they needed to talk immediately.

"I have something to tell you that I wish I didn't have to," she said when they sat down. "I'm totally ashamed of what I did, and you have every right to be furious."

Perry stared at her. "What're you talking about? What could possibly be so wrong?"

"The fact that you trust me implicitly only makes this worse," moaned Landa. She went on to explain exactly what happened the night before. She gave Perry a chance to ask for any more details, and ended by saying, "I want nothing more than to be with you. You mean the world to me. But I won't blame you if you decide to call off our relationship."

Perry was shocked, and he needed time to process what had happened. But in the days that followed, he saw that the old boyfriend was not actually a threat to their relationship. He appreciated that Landa was truthful in admitting her mistake, one she never intended to repeat. Nor did she repeat it.

In fact, it was in part what they learned from this early transgression that led the couple to develop their method for mutual monitoring of each other's drinking. Now, years later, they sometimes make jokes based on what happened. "Don't leave me alone with that handsome boss of yours," Landa might tease.

"Oh, I'll be glued to your side," Perry quips. "I'll probably get fired for lewd conduct."

Because they know without a shadow of a doubt how strong their couple bubble is now, they can laugh freely.

# SEVENTH GUIDING PRINCIPLE

The seventh principle in this book is that *partners should prevent each other from being a third wheel when relating to outsiders.* Every couple will find themselves engaging with outsiders, so your best bet is to rely on a strong and intact couple bubble. When you are solid with each other, the presence of thirds can actually amplify the positive aspects of your relationship. We saw how Landa and Perry have done this.

Here are some supporting principles to guide you:

1. Always make your partner number one. And say and do things—little ones and big ones—that remind your partner this is so. If your partner feels confident he or she is number one in your eyes, it will be much harder for thirds to pose a threat. The problem is that we often assume our partner already knows they're number one and doesn't need

reminders. But you know what they say happens when people *ass-u-me* something, right? They make an ass out of you and me!

2. Don't shy away from thirds. It might be tempting to reason that if thirds can cause trouble in a twosome relationship, it would be best to stay clear of them. Obviously, this wouldn't work in the case of children and in-laws. But it doesn't work for other outsiders, either. Our friends and other activities greatly enrich our lives. The key is not to avoid them or minimize contact, but to find healthy ways to bring them into your twosome.

   You might wonder, what if my partner and I don't share the same level of interest in a particular third? In fact, this is likely to occur. With the exception of your children, most outside people or interests probably are associated with one of you more than with the other. But this doesn't matter. Remember, as we discussed in chapter 6, you have agreed to be there for your partner. This means being there at that less-than-thrilling annual office party. It means going to the movie you consider sappy or boring or a bit too violent. Or to that baseball or football or soccer or basketball or hockey game. Why? Because—at the risk of sounding like that proverbial broken record—you're doing it for your partner. And your partner does the same for you.

   And if you still can't find it in you to enjoy the friend or party or movie or game, concentrate on your partner, and on enjoying your partner's enjoyment.

3. Realize that you as a couple hold power. In fairy tales, it is always said that if the King and Queen are living happily, then all is well across the land. If they're at odds, suffering is inevitable in their land. The same principle holds true in your household. If you and your partner are unified and secure with one another, your children, extended family, guests, and even pets will naturally attune to you. How you are with each other will rub off on them. It will be the two of you, and not any thirds, who set the tone when you're all together. Everyone benefits from a couple who are secure in their bubble.

# CHAPTER 8

# Fighting Well: How to Win by Letting Your Partner Win, Too

In chapter 2, I stated that the brain is wired first and foremost for war. Admittedly, a scary proposition, but one I think it's fair to say science supports. The fact is, we all have primitives, and our primitives often are itching for a fight.

The balance you and your partner strike on a day-to-day—even moment-to-moment—basis between your primitives and ambassadors plays an important role in determining whether you remain loving with one another or go to war. It may be tempting to think that if you just get that balance right, all will be peaches and cream. You'll live in a state of perpetual peace: no disagreements, no arguments, no animosity, no fights.

Sorry to disappoint you, but that's simply not realistic. In fact, if a couple tell me they have never fought, I am immediately suspicious. It's true that partners who have created a couple bubble may fight less frequently or less intensely because they know the importance of putting their relationship before all other matters. These matters include thirds, as discussed in the previous chapter, as well as a range of self-interests, such as being right or looking good in the eyes of others. Although there is nothing inherently wrong with these self-interests, they can compete with the interests of the relationship. Even a secure couple bubble won't create complete immunity from discord.

So, a successful partnership doesn't indicate that a couple have figured out how to avoid all fights; rather, it shows that they have undertaken any necessary rewiring and become adept at the art of fighting well.

This sounds like a paradox. And it is. I can honestly say that if you learn to fight well, you and your partner will be happier together, and your relationship will feel more secure. Instead of destroying your couple bubble, fighting well will strengthen it. Of all the aspects covered in the ownership manual to your relationship, this probably is the most key to your survival!

In this chapter, we look at various techniques for fighting well, including waving the flag of friendliness at the appropriate time, staying in the play zone, being adept at reading your partner, not sweeping anything under the rug, and generally fighting smart.

# NIP A FIGHT IN THE BUD

Before we consider how to fight well, we might consider what it takes to avoid a fight. As I just said, it's not important to avoid all fights. Still, there is nothing wrong with nipping the unnecessary ones in the bud.

## WAVE THE FLAG OF FRIENDLINESS

One of the best ways partners can avoid war, especially when distress is mounting, is to quickly wave the flag of friendliness. You can do it. Your partner can do it. It doesn't really matter; all it takes is one person to make the first move.

As you recall, the smart vagus is one of the most important ambassadors when it comes to avoiding war. The smart vagus not only allows us to take a deep breath before acting, but also helps us modulate our voice to signal friendliness. Take that extra second before you speak to be aware of the tone and volume of your voice. Our other ambassadors, particularly the orbitofrontal cortex—which, you'll recall, allows us to step into someone else's shoes—can calm down our amygdalae before they scream red alert over what is actually a nonexistent threat. Make it clear you understand where your partner is coming from, and open the door to a friendly discussion about your respective points of view. Using a familiar term of endearment shows that your love hasn't been lost in the scuffle. Yet other ambassadors specialize in helping us produce facial expressions that can ease our partner's distress. An unequivocal smile can communicate goodwill more rapidly than any words.

Sound silly? I don't think so. In chapter 4, we saw how Paul and Barbara used a smile or a look or a grasp of the hand to calm each other's primitives and communicate support. You can try this technique at any point, though it may not always be effective in the midst of a heated dispute. Nevertheless, many a war has been avoided with a friendly smile, a well-placed touch, and a reassuring voice.

## IT'S ALL JUST BLAH-BLAH-BLAH

When you wave the flag of friendliness, you in essence take a shortcut. You circumvent all the angry words that make up a fight, and instead communicate with a single gesture. The same can hold true in the midst of a fight. Sometimes when you have reached an apparent impasse, the most effective thing you or your partner can do is just…shut up.

I mean that literally. Stop speaking. Recognize that your primitives are threatened, and nothing of interpersonal value can come out of your mouth until your ambassadors are back online.

As you recall, our left brain is wired to be highly verbal and logical. It specializes in processing detailed information and readily engages with all the minutiae that go into an argument. At its best, it can sort out the minutiae and settle the argument; at its worst—directed by the primitives, most notably the amygdalae—it produces a lot of blah-blah-blah. What comes out of threatened partners' mouths is garbage, useless blather whose only purpose is to fend off attack or aggression. It's as if both brains are interacting amygdalae to amygdalae, with no evidence of flexibility, complexity, creativity, or contingency. What you say in this situation will only need to be discounted later, when you and your partner attempt to deal with all the hurtful things your amygdalae did to one another.

So, what I'm suggesting is that you shift your partner toward friendliness and away from threat. If you can do this, you will have aborted a fight.

---

## Exercise: Catch Yourselves in the Blah-Blah-Blah

Next time you and your partner are locked in a fight, see if you can turn it around by catching the blah-blah-blah.

1. Talk with your partner ahead of time, and agree that one or the other of you will catch the blah-blah-blah and make the appropriate correction. It is important that you agree beforehand and each take responsibility for changing course, not simply calling the other out.

2. When a fight occurs, pay attention to how you are speaking to one another. If you find that you're fighting over who said what when, or how one of you is like he or she was years ago and has never changed, or how someone else agrees that the other partner is a schmoe (aka jerk), then you are engaged in the blah-blah-blah of warfare. Time to stop.

3. Now make the appropriate correction. For example, you might wave the flag of friendliness ("Okay, I'm not helping the situation here"). Or move forward and touch your partner lovingly and say, "I'm sorry, I'm making this worse" or "I love you and I shouldn't be bringing all this other stuff up."

4. Once you have corrected, don't go back to the blah-blah-blah. Instead, condense your bottom-line point and tell it to your partner in one short sentence. Reason? The primitives can't process complex phrases, and the ambassadors aren't fully home yet. So keep your verbal communication short and sweet (emphasis on sweet). Remember to attend to what works for your partner, not simply what works for you!

---

# Staying in the Play Zone

I find in my work with couples that many partners who don't know how to fight well did not learn how to engage in rough-and-tumble play during childhood. Rough-and-tumble play is extremely important for both boys and girls.

All mammals use rough-and-tumble play, especially when very young. Humans are unique in that our earliest play takes place with our primary caregiver, at close range, using our eyes and voice. Mothers and babies can play endlessly, chattering, cooing and making other sounds while maintaining mutual gaze. Mice, kittens, and puppies don't do this. They simply rough-and-tumble. They may appear locked in battle, but it's all in good fun—without any declared winners or losers.

Rough-and-tumble play for humans generally comes later, often with a sibling who helps us discover our strength and our impact on another's body. We learn how hard to push and pull, how to tell the other person not to push or pull so hard, and so on. A certain degree of competitive spirit may be present, but it's still all in good fun. As youngsters, anchors often are freer in their play than are islands and waves, who tend to be held in check by their insecurities. This pattern can continue into later life.

## THE LESSON OF PLAY: NO ONE IS A LOSER

Learning how to play well as children helps us fight well as adults. Secure couples know that a good fight stays within the play zone. By that, I mean the fight isn't allowed to get ugly. A sense of playfulness is maintained, and a tone of friendliness. Play, after all, is fun. When we invoke the spirit of play, there is no need for anyone to declare victory, and no one is made a loser.

How do you do this? Essentially, it's your ambassadors who will save the day. Because if the army of primitives gains the upper hand, well, then it's war, baby!

So it's up to you and your partner to listen to your ambassadors. Their message goes something like this: "We're okay. Everyone will survive. Just relax! You're in love with each other, remember? Your relationship won't be in jeopardy because of this fight."

Heeding this message can, in effect, rewire the tendency to be geared first and foremost toward war. You and your partner can develop a system of communication that includes ways to hold your primitives at bay and make sure any fights take place on friendly ground. In chapter 7, we saw how Landa and Perry used a private language to communicate in front of thirds. What I'm suggesting here is similar. You can't count on knowing how to be playful during a fight if you haven't laid the groundwork beforehand. So talk about how you want to feel and communicate when a fight does occur. Build on the ways you play together. Become more familiar with the nods and winks (or whatever signals work for you) that you use with each other when no disagreement is present, and learn to trust them when tensions arise, as well.

If you really trust that neither of you will end up a loser, you can feel more relaxed about the rough-and-tumble of fighting. You sense when to pursue and when to retreat. To less secure individuals, the prospect of retreat implies taking a loss or giving up one's stance. It implies defeat, maybe even humiliating defeat. Not so for secure couples. They know they're in it for the long haul, so they feel free to keep their guard down, even while fighting.

---

## EXERCISE: COME PLAY WITH ME!

When is the last time you and your partner engaged in rough-and-tumble play? Maybe...never? Well, it's time to roll up your sleeves and remove all sharp objects!

1. Find a safe place where you can both move around freely and not risk injury. An outdoor lawn can work, or a king-size bed or a soft carpet or even a large exercise mat.

2. Set some ground rules before you begin. For example, if either yells, "Time out!" both of you must stop instantly. If there is anything—for example, being held upside down—that doesn't feel safe, agree at the get-go that no one will do this.

3. Get down on the bed (or mat or carpet or lawn) together and play. You can push and pull, roll and curl up. Make all the sounds you want, but try not to talk because that will distract you from paying close attention to your physicality. You can analyze things later, if you must.

---

# READING YOUR PARTNER

One of the key elements to fighting well is being able to read your partner, to know in any given moment what he or she is feeling, thinking, and intending.

We may not be consciously aware when something is amiss, but we often can feel it in our bodies. We just don't quite feel right somehow. Probably the most reliable way to read a partner, however, is to use our visual acuity. When we look at our partner, our eyes rapidly and continuously take in information: moistness in his or her eyes, a slight flinch, the hint of a smile, a curling of the lips. Even the most subtle cues are quickly passed along—first to the primitives and then to the ambassadors. The amygdalae, as we saw in chapter 2, play a vital role in this process.

Couples in distress often look away from one another. This is a big mistake. The loss of continuous eye contact pulls each partner out of real-time tracking of one another and shifts each into a more internal, static, and historical perspective. Averting their eyes deprives the ambassadors of vital information and allows the primitives to take over. When this happens, each partner in effect moves away from the other—even if it's not a physical move—and into a state of high alert. At other times, the mistake is simply due to poor physical positioning. When partners aren't face to face in relatively close proximity (no more than about three feet apart), it is more difficult to accurately read one another. A minor issue can escalate quickly into a major problem when partners talk while driving or while walking side by side. (We saw this with Leia and Franklin, who fought in the car in chapter 2.) For this reason, I recommend against couples talking about important or emotional matters unless they can maintain eye contact and read each other's cues. Why give the amygdalae unnecessary power?

Of course, it can be tempting to pick up the phone when you want to work something out with your partner. You don't want to have to wait until you meet again in person. I can't stress enough: This is a bad idea! Hearing your partner's voice without the benefit of eyesight can be very misleading. If your or your partner's primitives go on high alert, there could be an early rush to war that could have been prevented if one of you read a more loving message on the other's face. Voices, and especially words, can be insufficient when primitives are on the warpath.

## THE PERILS OF DIGITAL FIGHTING

An even worse idea is e-mailing or text messaging. Many couples rely on these technologies, and of course they have great value when it comes to maintaining a 24/7 agreement, as we noted in chapter 6. But beware when a disagreement or potential disagreement is in the air. I have seen countless couples get into trouble texting about sensitive issues because they can't read each other's tone, intention, or feeling.

Consider Jill and Carol, both twenty-five, who love to use text messaging throughout the week. Both graduate students, they maintain a tether with one another through their cell phones. This is enjoyable when they both feel good as individuals and as a couple, but their texts can tear the tether and become drumbeats of war whenever either feels insecure. Even their emoticons can be misread as hostile and warlike.

For example, here is a text exchange that led to problems:

*Jill:* need ur lovin right now

*Carol:* can't talk

*Jill:* can't talk? not asking to *talk*

*Carol:* what?!

*Jill:* forget it

*Carol:* i'm in a meeting. talk later

*Jill:* can't talk later. see ya when i see ya ;)

*Carol:* ok, this is getting me angry. what's the ;) about?

*Jill:* gotta go

Because Carol thought Jill was giving her the brush-off, she ended up missing their dinner date. In her mind, she was waiting for Jill to clear up what she meant in her text. However, because it is easy to misinterpret or overlook emotions communicated in e-mails or texts, Jill didn't realize she had upset her partner, and subsequently forgot all about the exchange. By the time they were face-to-face later that evening, both their primitives were loaded, cocked, and ready to fire.

Carol and Jill could avoid these fights if they lessened their reliance on text messaging. If they continue texting, they need to understand the importance of immediately sending a strong message of friendliness, whether through texting, calling, or making an appointment to see one another as soon as possible.

---

## EXERCISE: READ ME

This exercise is similar to the Emote Me Game in chapter 4. Only this time, you take turns reading each other's emotions.

1. Ask your partner to pick an emotion and "get into it," but without speaking or engaging in any major physical activity. Your partner's job is to convey the emotion through the expression on his or her face, through posture, or through hand gestures. But nothing else.

2. Your job is to read your partner's emotion. See how close you can get to the specific emotion.

3. Then switch roles. You pick an emotion and enact it, and your partner will try to read you.

4. You may want to start with simple emotions: angry, happy, sad, afraid, surprised. If you want a more challenging game, try more subtle or complex emotions: for example, disappointed, rejected, relieved, disdainful, jealous, guilty, ashamed, helpless, trusting.

---

# FIGHTING SMART

So far we've talked about how fighting well involves making sure our ambassadors are managing our primitives. If you can do this—really do it, regardless of whether your partner is doing it in the moment or not—the odds of your relationship enduring are high.

But you deserve more than mere endurance: you deserve a relationship that is thriving. For this reason, partners in a relationship based on mutuality also have to take responsibility for managing one another's primitives. Remember the smart vagus and dumb vagus? The smart one keeps us socially engaged, and the dumb one doesn't. Each partner wants to make sure the other's smart vagus is operating properly, along with the rest of the ambassadors. Make sure you breathe, relax your muscles, and mind your tone of voice. In effect, you pool the resources of your ambassadors. If one person is having a bad day, the other steps up. And vice versa. You track each other's moods. In a heated dispute, you pay attention to how much is too much and how long is too long. You know when to quit or when to change the subject or distract one another. Sometimes it's best to give things a rest so you both have a chance to cool off. However, don't just leave the room, hang up, or turn away. If you do that, your partner may interpret your actions as dismissive. Rather, make sure the time out is mutually acceptable—say, twenty to thirty minutes to cool off—and not unilateral. Taking responsibility in this way is what I call *smart fighting*.

Smart fighting is of the ambassadors, by the ambassadors, and for the ambassadors. It ensures that they will still be standing at the end. Remember, only ambassadors can be influenced, persuaded, cajoled, or seduced. Primitives aren't concerned with maintaining relationships; all they care about is not being killed. Therefore, your and your partner's primitives better not be the only ones left standing at the end of a fight.

Couples who fight smart seek an outcome that allows both partners to be winners. They aim for a win-win solution. They say to each other, "We both have to feel good about this," or "I'll be happy only if you're happy, too," or "We're in this together." At the same time, they aren't afraid to tell each other: "We are okay, but what just happened is not," or "You're a dear, but I'm going to get my way on this one," or "I love you, but you're being a pain in the ass today and I think you know it." They can say all this because their ambassadors know how to wave the flag of friendliness and how to make sure no one strays out of the play zone.

# GOOD FOR ME, GOOD FOR YOU

So many of the couples I see in my therapy practice come with expectations that each partner should know certain things about how relationships ought to work. It's almost as if partners expect each other to come to the table pretrained. It doesn't dawn on them that they must train one another to do things or continue to parent one another in ways their real parents failed. Expecting your partner to share your values at all times, and in all ways, leads to great disillusionment, disappointment, and anger.

"You should *want* to do this for me!" one partner explains to the other, trying to persuade him or her.

"But nobody does that!" another partner asserts in an attempt to dissuade the other from doing this or that.

"I didn't marry you for *this*!" says yet another, in attempt to correct a partner's moral compass.

In all of these instances, the partners are trying to assert their will to get the other to do what they want him or her to do. They speak as if a truly mutual agreement is in place. But if you listen closely, it isn't hard to see that they are actually expressing self-interests under the guise of what should be good for the relationship. Often, this amounts to nothing short of bullying.

There is a better way. Instead of using fear or threat to manipulate one another into doing or not doing something, you can use positive influence. Remember, the owner's manual to your relationship provides a wealth of information about your partner's predilections. You can use this information in the best way—for good, not evil. In this case, good means what is good for both of you. Self-interests will still exist, but they are folded into the greater good of the relationship, such that, when a fight occurs, nobody loses and everybody wins.

Let's examine how this could work for one couple.

## SEEKING A FAIR DEAL

Donna and Sean, a couple in their fifties, are invited to a fancy social event at the high-tech company where Donna works. Donna is always asking Sean to join her at these types of events, and he is always resisting. Sean, a landscape designer, hates going to these things and makes no bones about it. A part of Donna feels that Sean's resistance is unloving, and that if he really cares for her, he'd understand how important these events are to her career. Sean feels that Donna's insistence that he attend even though he feels bored among her engineer colleagues is insensitive and unloving. If she really cares about him, she'd let him off the hook.

Let's take a look at several ways the couple can handle this situation.

### SCENARIO 1

Donna becomes furious as Sean rolls his eyes at her request. "I don't think this is fair," she complains. "We said we'd support one another in our work, and this is my work. You're not being very supportive."

"Well, you're not being supportive of me and my feelings," replies Sean, who's been down this road many times. "You know how much I hate these things, and being forced to go feels unfair to me. How come when I ask for things, you're able to say no, but I don't have the same rights?"

"What do you mean? I always do what you want," Donna objects, pouting. "We're always going to your stupid movies."

"Thanks a lot! I didn't know you considered my movies stupid. Besides, we see what you want, too. We're always seeing your dumb chick flicks."

"You know what? Just forget it!" says Donna, exasperated, "I'll go by myself." And she walks out of the room.

After a few moments pass, Sean shouts, "Okay! I'll do it."

From another room, Donna shouts back, "Don't do me any favors, and I won't do any for you, either, okay?"

At the last minute, Sean ends up going. Donna is relieved not to go alone. At the same time, she feels an underlying anxiety. She will certainly pay for this.

## SCENARIO 2

Donna notices Sean's discontent with her invitation. She's tired of the effort it takes to get him to go with her, so this time she says, "You know, I have to be at that shindig tonight. I can go alone. You do whatever you want."

Sean looks at her in surprise. "Really? You mean that?"

Donna replies after a short pause, "Sure."

"Cool!" says Sean.

Later, as Donna is leaving for the event, she sees Sean ensconced on the couch, watching his favorite television show. He's happy, but she clearly is not. "Well then, bye," she says abruptly, without giving him a hug or kiss.

"Bye!" he calls after her, disregarding her blatant cues of unhappiness. "Have a great time! I'll be here, waiting." Though he is glad he's off the hook, Sean can't escape the feeling he will pay for this later.

## SCENARIO 3

Sean states strongly, "I really, really, really don't want to go to this thing tonight."

"I understand, I really do," replies Donna. "But this is very important to me."

"It's always important to you, Donna," counters Sean. "What about me? Are my feelings important to you?"

"Of course they are," says Donna. "Okay, how can I make this worth your while?"

"What do you mean?" asks Sean, surprised.

Donna sits down next to Sean so she can look into his eyes. "How about this? If you go with me tonight, tomorrow we'll go see that action movie you've been wanting to see."

Sean thinks for a moment, raising his eyebrows to signal he's considering the idea. "That's pretty good, but I think I need something more than that," he replies.

Now it's Donna's turn to think. "Okay," she says after a moment, "how's this? Tonight I'll leave the party whenever you want, as long as I can make my rounds and not leave conspicuously. And when we get home, I'll tickle your back for twenty minutes."

"A full twenty minutes?" Sean smiles widely. "You've got a deal!"

Donna smiles back. "But," she says, with her index finger pointed upward, "you can't complain for the entire evening. Do we still have a deal?"

"Deal!" responds Sean, who then kisses her and pulls her down on the couch with him.

They both leave for the event feeling happy, and neither will look back on this as an unfair deal.

## HOUSEKEEPING FOR THE COUPLE BUBBLE

I think it's obvious which scenario is preferable. Really, the third is the only fair solution. But so many couples swing between scenarios 1 and 2: either one partner or the other gets the raw end of the deal. This is because they don't know the basic rules for negotiating within a couple bubble.

Of course, it's only natural that partners won't always view things the same way or want to do the same thing at any given time. Not everyone loves action movies, for example, and not everyone loves office parties. You may want to spend money on an expensive meal, while your partner would rather save up for a longer vacation trip. You may be in the mood to see your partner's family one time, but not in a mood the next time. Fair enough. My point is that none of this should be a problem.

And it won't be if you learn to negotiate effectively. In a nutshell, (1) your negotiations don't have to be entirely symmetrical, (2) bargaining is fine, and (3) any compromises you make should not result in one person losing.

Think of this process as good housekeeping for your couple bubble.

Next time a fight is in the offing, instead of expecting your partner to function as your clone, put your collective energies into making sure the solution feels meaningful and worthwhile for both of you. Keep at the negotiations until you reach that point. In essence, there can be no forward movement, no decision making, no action unless you and your partner agree the solution will work for both of you.

We got a glimpse of this process in scenario 3. In it, Donna and Sean negotiated as anchors. By contrast, when an island faces a situation in which each partner wants to do something different, the only apparent solution is to go their separate ways. We saw this in scenario 2. On the other hand, as we saw in scenario 1, one partner can bully the other into submission. This is the way of the wave.

If you and your partner reach a point where you still aren't both satisfied with a solution, some compensation or repair may need to take place. This can be tricky, especially when past experiences of inequity, unfairness, injustice, and insensitivity color the present situation. I said negotiations don't have to be symmetrical, in the sense that one or the other of you may appear to give up more at any particular moment; however, over the long run, any inequities need to balance out. Sticking to the principle of "good for me, good for you" should prevent either of you from keeping a tally against the other.

# OVER THE LONG HAUL

Some issues between partners can be resolved, if not immediately, then eventually. Other matters may never be resolved, and may always be a source of potential conflict. In fact, because no two brains are alike, the chance of two people agreeing on everything is slim to nil. For this reason, John Gottman, a researcher and marital expert, believes that couples don't need to solve all their unresolved conflicts, but they do need to deal effectively with these issues (Gottman and Silver 2004). And I would agree. Couples who are in it for the long haul know how to play and fight well, remain fearlessly confident in the resilience of their relationship, and don't try to avoid conflict.

# NOTHING SWEPT UNDER THE RUG

Dennis and Kathleen are expert fighters. They pay close attention to one another, especially when talking about topics that are important to or sensitive for either of them. They have a policy never to avoid anything, no matter how difficult. Neither partner feels afraid of becoming overwhelmed or of being shut down by the other when they fight. Nor does either give indirect messages to the other about controversial matters, such as complaints and the like. If Kathleen needs to bring up something to Dennis that she knows he won't like, she does so quickly and without ceremony. It's a kind of friendly hit-and-run, a strategy both have agreed works for them.

For instance, both are at dinner alone one evening talking about general niceties, nothing stressful. Suddenly, while looking into Dennis's eyes, Kathleen says, "We have to talk about your job situation." She's referring to Dennis's recent demotion at work and his promise to find another position. She knows this is going to cause a shame reaction.

Dennis lowers his head, breaking eye contact with Kathleen. "I know. Do we have to talk about this right now?"

"No," she says quickly, "but we *are* going to talk about it, okay?" Then she changes the subject.

Dennis quickly recovers, and they continue to have a pleasant dinner.

Later that evening, while getting ready for bed, Kathleen says, "About your job . . ."

Dennis sighs and says, "Oh, geez. Come on, honey, I don't want to talk about it *now*."

Kathleen kisses him and looks into his eyes. "Sweetheart, I know you don't want to talk about this, but we can't avoid it forever. Bring it up with me tomorrow, or I will, okay?"

"Okay," he says, smiling back at her.

And the conversation does take place the following day. Dennis's feelings about his job aren't fully resolved, and it still is hard for him to talk about this topic. However, no one can doubt that this couple are there to support one another. They don't avoid important matters simply because they feel bad or expect a bad reaction. Rather, as we discussed in chapter 4, they are competent managers of one another and know how to shift, soothe, influence, and inspire each other. It's clear they're in it for the long haul. So any fights that occur are only minor speed bumps on the road for them.

# REMEMBER THE GOOD, FORGET THE BAD

If your partner tends to remind you of things you have done to injure him or her, chances are your response is along the lines of "Why do you always remember such things? Why can't you just forget?"

You want to move on. But does it ever occur to you that you helped create that memory in the first place by not doing anything to fix it in time?

Any intense feeling—positive or negative—that stays in our awareness for too long will be transferred into long-term memory. The ambassadors, notably the hippocampus, are responsible for converting short-term memories into long-term ones. As a primitive concerned with our safety and security, the amygdalae make sure we don't forget painful memories. In this way, grudges are formed.

If you're in it for the long haul, it behooves you and your partner to avoid creating and maintaining grudges. Do this by allowing your ambassadors to overrule your primitives. Fix your bad memories so they become good memories. Kathleen did this by insisting Dennis talk with her about his job. If she had let it go when he was reluctant to talk, they might both have had bad memories: for Dennis, it would have centered on the job itself, and for Kathleen it would have been about her husband withdrawing from her because he was too mired in depression.

The idea is to transform bad memories into good ones before they enter long-term memory as grudges. However, it's possible to transform a bad memory even years later. I'm not suggesting long-standing grudges will disappear with a snap of your fingers, but if you and your partner are willing to do the work, you can get past them.

---

# EXERCISE: THE GRATEFULNESS INVENTORY

This exercise is derived from Naikan, the Japanese art of self-reflection. It can be difficult to do, especially if you're a wave, but it is well worth the effort. Take at least thirty minutes to do this exercise.

1. On a piece of paper, make three columns.

2. At the top of column 1, write, "What he/she gave me." List everything your partner has given you in the last week. Be specific and concrete—for

example, "He made me pancakes for breakfast yesterday," not "He does the cooking." Don't move on until you've listed everything your partner gave you—even the expected things. Fact is, you got those, too,

3. At the top of the next column write, "What I gave him/her." You can spend less time laboring over this column. Nevertheless, be specific and concrete.

4. Label the last column "The trouble I caused him/her." You might ask why there isn't a fourth column for the trouble your partner caused you. Because you probably already know this all too well. As with the first column, do this thoroughly. And be honest: whether you intend to or not, you cause trouble and can be burdensome to your partner.

5. Now study your finished inventory. If you did it correctly, the first and third columns should be longer than the second one. Notice in particular what you receive from your partner, but tend to take for granted.

6. You might find yourself inclined to write a letter of gratitude for three things your partner gave you. You might even feel compelled to write a letter of apology for three things you did to cause your partner grief. And finally, you might want to share this entire list with your partner. If all goes well, your partner may want to do this exercise in return.

# Eighth Guiding Principle

The eighth principle in this book is that *partners who want to stay together must learn to fight well.* When you and your partner are relating within a strong and secure couple bubble, fights don't threaten your partnership. You are able to pick up on each other's distress cues and manage them posthaste. You don't ignore problems and let them fester. Rather, you quickly error correct, repair, or wave the flag of friendliness.

Here are some supporting principles to guide you:

1. Losing is not allowed. Of course, no one wants to lose. I'm sure you and your partner are no exceptions. At times, it may be tempting to

assert your will, to try to pick up a few wins for yourself. But honestly, what value will your pro-self interests have if a fight results in your partner being knocked out, on tilt, or otherwise non–compos mentis? Not much. That would be a Pyrrhic victory.

So, you have to retrain yourselves. You have to rewire your ways of fighting. Think in terms of defusing conflict that turns ugly, rather than necessarily resolving it entirely. Most importantly, when you fight, both of you have to win...or you will both lose. And that's not an acceptable outcome.

2. Giving up isn't allowed, either. Let me be clear: smart fighting is not about abdicating your position or giving up your self-interests. It's about wrestling with your partner, engaging without hesitation or avoidance, and at the same time being willing to relax your own position. You go back and forth with each other, until the two of you come up with something that's good for both of you. You take what you each bring to the table and, with it, create something new that provides mutual relief and satisfaction.

3. Every fight brings a new day. In asking you to fight well, I'm asking your ambassadors to rule over your primitives. We all know that can be tough, and even more so in the midst of battle. So don't expect 100 percent success at your first try. If the minute a conversation overheats, you forget everything I've said, don't give up. Try again tomorrow.

# CHAPTER 9

# Love Is Up Close:
# How to Rekindle Love
# Through Eye Contact

In the last chapter, we looked at what it takes to fight well and keep yourself from going to war with your partner. Couples who don't know how to do this find themselves in a state of heightened alert not only during fights, but sometimes long after a specific battle has ended. Verbally they may have called a truce, but under cover their amygdalae are primed and ready to go at a moment's notice. It's as if they're permanently wired for war, with no hope of rewiring. Other couples may have learned to fight in ways that leave both partners still standing at the end. They know how to read one another, how to wave the flag of friendliness, and when to recall the troops. All this serves to keep them on a relatively even keel. But ultimately these couples, too, will fall short if their love hits a low point and they aren't able to rekindle it. It's one thing to fight well, and something else altogether to love well.

In this chapter, we look at how to use your ambassadors and your primitives to make love not war. This is the ultimate rewiring. And it's not as difficult as you might think. After all, you and your partner already know what it's like to feel intimately connected. More than likely, that bright spark of love is what brought you together in the first place. All you need is to become acquainted with ways to rekindle the fire when   or even before—it starts to grow dim.

# LUST IS AT A DISTANCE

I often tell couples who are striving to recreate and hold onto a more intimate connection that lust is at a distance, but love is up close. I advise them not to confuse the two, and not to depend on lust to rekindle their romance. This is a mistake too many couples make.

## BECOMING STRANGERS

Consider Viktor and Tatiana, both fifty-five years old. Their two children, twins, recently left for college, and the couple find themselves with more time alone together than they've had in years. Initially Tatiana looked forward to the romantic vacation they'd promised each other. However, after a few weeks, her enthusiasm gave way to an unexpected anxiety. Somehow, when the kids were around every day, she had failed to notice the distance that had developed between her and Viktor. Mealtime conversations revolved around school activities, sports, and homework. It was easy to overlook her husband's minimal role in these interactions. Besides, he was always preoccupied with work: it was hard to imagine him without a cell phone glued to his ear, even at the dinner table.

Only now, with just the two of them at home, is Tatiana fully realizing the degree to which their intimacy is lacking. It's not as if they're fighting or arguing. There is nothing obviously "wrong." Well, except perhaps for the infrequency with which they have sex. But even that has never been officially acknowledged as a problem by either of them. In fact, Viktor often declares his love by sending his wife flowers and fancy gifts, something he has done throughout their marriage because he wants her to feel he is perpetually wooing her.

Tatiana decides to talk to Viktor to see if they can plan a vacation that might rekindle the romance in their relationship. Because she knows he's excited about their upcoming trip and sees it as romantic, she doesn't want to come off as too critical or disparaging.

"Have you given more thought to where we should go?" she asks tentatively one evening, as they get up from the dinner table, having exchanged only a few words during the meal.

Viktor's face lights up as he turns to her and thrusts his cell phone into his pocket. "I say we get a penthouse suite in downtown Manhattan. We've always talked about being right in center of the action. We can do matinees in the afternoon, dancing in the evening, the best restaurants, the museums—"

Tatiana stops him. "Yes, we've talked about that, and it could be amazing," she says. "But we also talked about Maine, and a cabin with a fireplace. What do you think about something more intimate, like that?"

Viktor scrunches up his face. "Honey," he exclaims, "this is *our* trip, no expenses barred. We've taken the kids to plenty of cabins!" He laughs, then grabs her and waltzes her around the living room. "Just wait, I'll show you the time of your life!"

Tatiana senses her husband's genuine enthusiasm and doesn't want to disappoint him. She tells herself a quiet retreat in Maine could bode disaster if it only accentuates the distance between them. At the same time, she can't help feeling an extravagant vacation without a free moment to spare isn't what they need to get back on track with each other.

This is a couple without the ability to continually rekindle their love. It's not even clear to both of them that the fire has gone out, let alone why. They treat one another almost as strangers. Viktor goes so far as to intentionally cultivate a sense of unfamiliarity, believing it has the power to generate lust and provide a certain thrill. Yes, this couple has made it through twenty years of marriage without considering divorce. But any excitement they feel these days is tepid because it is based on a love that exists only at a distance. They have settled for that because they don't know what it would take to have love up close.

## THE PRIMITIVES' APPRAISAL: SEEKING FAMILIARITY

Of course, partners aren't always up close. At least, we don't start off that way. At the beginning of courtship, as new lovers, we generally first meet at a distance. We visually appraise one another according to a variety of factors: gross physical anatomy, apparel, grooming, hair color, and so on.

Our brain plays an important role in this process. It relies on different senses to gather information about people in our environment, depending on whether they're at a distance or close to us. When you see someone across the room, for instance, you use your far visual system (which some refer to as the *dorsal visual stream*) to track if he or she remains still or moves toward or away from you. This visual system works in tandem with your amygdalae and other primitives to determine whether the person is safe or unsafe, attractive or unattractive, and whether you want him or her to approach. Remember, our primitives' main objective is to not be killed. Beyond that, they are invested in perpetuating the species. For this reason, they are experts in detecting the potential for lust, and do it best from a distance.

When it comes to mate selection, our brain prefers a simple neurobiological load; in other words, it prefers familiarity. A person who appears too unfamiliar is likely to create a complex load and thus repel our primitives. Too much stranger-ness is threatening. (I use the term *stranger-ness*—as opposed to strangeness, meaning weirdness—to refer to the quality of being like a stranger.) Familiarity with just the right amount of stranger-ness to spice things up can cause an attraction that brings us into closer physical proximity. Then, at close range, our ambassadors have a chance to become engaged and begin the process of psychobiological vetting to determine whether this person meets our criteria for a long-term relationship.

In the end, romantic love must pass muster with both our primitives and our ambassadors. Lust only has to pass muster with our primitives.

# LOVE IS UP CLOSE

So, what exactly happens when two people are in close proximity? What makes the sparks—and I don't mean just lustful sparks—fly? I think it's worthwhile to examine the neurobiological dynamics that come into play when we first fall in love, because these same processes are the key to rekindling love throughout the relationship.

## THE AMBASSADORS' APPRAISAL: CLOSE AND PERSONAL

Most notably, as we approach a potential partner, our near senses become engaged. These include first and foremost our close-up visual stream (which some refer to as the *ventral visual stream*), reserved for people or objects deemed safe and those being closely observed.

As you move toward another person and come within an approximate distance of two to three feet, you may find yourself hesitating as your brain adjusts to the near visual stream. Meeting another person in close proximity, your brain is predisposed to take in the face: the fine, smooth muscles of the face as they shift and change, the kaleidoscopic fluctuations in skin tone, the eyes dancing and pupils opening and closing in tune with your buzzing nervous systems as the two of you interact. You can see more detail in the face and body. A person looks quite different up close than at a distance.

Most of us initially scan the face in close range, focusing first on the mouth and then the eyes. Because our brain's right hemisphere specializes in social and emotional perception, we tend to look more at the other person's left eye (the right hemisphere is cross-connected to the left side of the body). Our gaze triangulates between the mouth and right and left eye, but we tend to focus on the left for cues about safety. There are, of course, many exceptions to this. People in some cultures, for example, consider direct eye contact impolite or inappropriate. Other individuals, independent of cultural influence, avoid eye contact either for safety concerns or because they find it easier to look for cues on the mouth or other parts of the body and are unable to pick up cues in the eyes.

Another near sense that engages in close proximity is our sense of smell. We appraise another's body odor on several levels, including but not only on the obvious level of perfumes, colognes, and soaps. We also can smell more subtle scents produced by the neuroendocrine system that suggest friendliness, sexual arousal, fear, and even dislike. We may engage in brief or sustained touch. We may even engage a variety of implicit sense perceptions that seem energetic and indescribable, as for example, when someone says, "I felt my heart beat strongly just by standing next to her."

## HOW WE FALL IN LOVE

We fall in love at close proximity. I mean real love, not the imagined kind that some can conjure up through fantasy or at a distance, or that is really just lust masquerading as love.

The eyes play an important role in igniting real love. When you gaze into your partner's eyes, you can see not only his or her essence, but the entire play of the nervous system. You can witness the live, exciting, and rapidly changing inner landscape of emotion, energy, and reality that belongs to and defines your partner.

It is an unavoidable fact that the body shows signs of deterioration as we age. The most obvious signs, such as changes in hair color, weight, posture, or agility, are apparent at a distance. Closer up, signs of aging include wrinkled skin and gnarled fingers. But have you noticed the one body part that seems miraculously immune to aging? The eyes! As long as we're mentally and emotionally healthy, they remain beautiful, vibrant, and vital. It's as though, through them, we have the means to fall in love permanently at our disposal.

A few minutes of sustained gazing can lead to relaxation, a sense of safety, and full here-and-now engagement. Attachment authority Daniel Stern (2004) terms this *moments of meeting*.

## MEETING AGAIN AND AGAIN

Kent and Sandra are in their fifties. They have been married for twenty-five years and have grown children who are now out of the home. Though each remains physically fit, neither has done anything radical to offset the natural aging process. Many of their friends have undergone plastic surgeries and injection treatments, but thus far this couple have resisted the peer pressure to remain unusually youthful.

Kent and Sandra realized early in their relationship that gazing into each other's eyes had the power to rekindle strong feelings of love. Kent says, "When I look into Sandy's eyes it's as if I'm meeting her for the first time all over again."

Sandra echoes that sentiment. "I never tire of looking at Kent. I see so much in his eyes, beyond anything I could put into words."

Recently, Kent and Sandra have noticed that friends who complain of boredom and dissatisfaction in their long-term relationships tend to avoid close gazing. These couples often talk and joke about lusting over strangers at a distance, as if that could solve their problems. Kent and Sandra wonder if the tedium their friends suffer isn't partly due to a lack of close gazing and the inability to rekindle love.

I would agree. In fact, it's easy for two people to settle into dulling familiarity when they are living off static notions of one another, notions that are easily maintained at a distance. When we look into one another's eyes close up, it becomes impossible to remain in a total state of familiarity. This is because at close range, as we looking into another's eyes, what we see is inherently strange and complex. We become aware of each other's stranger-ness, which makes us aware again of novelty and unpredictability. This allows for just enough familiarity and stranger-ness to rekindle love and excitement.

## EXERCISE: FROM NEAR TO FAR AND BACK

Try this exercise with your partner. You will need a large room or a large outdoor area where you can be alone together. I suggest doing this exercise when you meet each other at the end of the day, but you can do it at any time that's convenient to both of you.

1. Stand or sit in close proximity, no more than two feet apart. Ask your partner how his or her day was. As you listen and ask questions for clarification, pay attention to your partner's eyes. What cues do you glean from them? See if you can listen **and** attend to the eyes at the same time. Don't stare! Keep scanning your partner's eyes for information.

2. After a few minutes, before your partner has finished talking, move apart from each other. If possible, have at least twenty feet between you. Again, attend to your partner's eyes. Do you feel as connected as before?

3. Finally, conclude the conversation back in close proximity. This time, however, keep your eyes closed and use only your other near senses, such as smell and touch, and of course hearing.

4. Switch roles, and repeat steps 1 through 3 with your partner asking you about your day.

5. Compare notes. How did the experiences of relating close up (with eyes open and closed) and at a distance differ? At what moment did you feel most connected?

# UP CLOSE WITH ISLANDS AND WAVES

Some individuals, especially islands and waves, have trouble up close. They may not pick up important cues from their partner or simply not pick them up quickly enough, or may not know how to quickly fix misattuned moments. All is not lost, though, because if the wave or island's partner is what I have termed a competent manager of the other, he or she can make up for the other's deficits. It is not essential for both partners to be equally competent managers; however, if one is particularly bad at it, the other must be much better.

## REKINDLING WITH ISLANDS

Many islands experience some degree of difficulty with close-up interactions, although this may not be apparent during courtship. As their name suggests, islands tend to prefer gazing either inwardly or distantly.

We can look to their childhood to explain why this happens. Many islands did not experience a lot of physical contact as children, or did not receive the mixture of comfort and stimulation that comes from a parent gazing into an infant's eyes. Rather, the contact they did experience may have been overly intrusive or misattuned. As a result, many adult islands experience aversion at being what they perceive as too close to a partner. This aversion can include not only gazing, but the near senses of smell, taste, and touch. Many islands report feeling inexplicably irritated and even harassed by their partner's attempts to get near or to maintain close physical contact. They may feel at once intruded upon and ashamed of their aversive reactions, and may attempt to conceal it with avoidance, excuses, withdrawal, or anger.

Judd, an island, loved to gaze at Irene when they were dating in college. He fell in love with her deep green eyes. Her pupils always seemed wide open, as if guilelessly inviting him to merge with her. So beautiful, so engaging, so safe, he thought.

Two year into the marriage, something changed. He began to see her eyes as pushy, invasive, and meddling. Her pupils always seemed constricted, like little pinholes. He stopped gazing into her eyes. He preferred looking at her from afar, while she interacted with others. When she sought physical proximity, he felt annoyed. The sound of her voice aroused anger in him, and her touch sometimes made him bristle. He became oddly sensitive to the smell of her breath and her skin. He stopped enjoying their kisses and began to avoid anything but a brief peck on the lips.

Irene, herself an island, tried not to notice what was happening. She buried herself in work and convinced herself this was simply a natural phase for married couples; it was what people meant when they said, "The honeymoon is over."

Judd was in a panic. What, he asked himself, could have caused such a change in his sensorium? Had he fallen out of love? He certainly thought so. Because he avoided close contact with Irene, he had no way to rekindle feelings of love for her. He couldn't engender feelings of either stranger-ness or novelty with her. She became an overly familiar, if not familial, figure to him. At the same time, Judd found himself lusting for others at a distance. He engaged in occasional dalliances and one-night stands with women with whom he could relive the excitement and possibility of sex and romance, as he had done with Irene in the beginning. But whenever a woman became too demanding of continued involvement, his aversive reactions would reappear and he would quickly cut off all communication.

Judd was forced to admit his problem when Irene discovered his infidelities and kicked him out the house.

After two weeks of painful separation, Judd owned up to his mistakes and begged Irene for a second chance. Irene agreed to reconcile. Slowly, the couple started "dating" again. He once again enjoyed gazing into her deep green eyes. His near senses again delighted in her smell, taste, and touch. The sound of her voice warmed him as it had in the beginning. With his renewed sense of love for Irene, it wasn't hard to win his way back into the house. However, shortly thereafter, his aversions returned.

"What's wrong with me?" he worried silently day and night.

Fortunately, this time Irene recognized the problem and was able to convince Judd to go to couple therapy with her so they could address the more serious problems that were tough to solve on their own.

## REKINDLING WITH WAVES

Unlike islands, waves tend to be comfortable with their near senses and even crave physical proximity for long durations. Waves likely will not experience aversive reactions to a partner, unless they have a history of physical or sexual trauma, in which case they may be simultaneously adverse to the closeness they crave.

Because waves crave close contact, they can appear overly intrusive, even threatening, to their partner, especially if the partner is an island who is sensitive to approach. Waves may not be aware of the effect they have on their partner, and therefore not make an effort to correct their errors.

Unlike islands, waves tend to have experienced lots of physical contact as children and often report memories of a parent gazing into their eyes. In courtship, a wave's come-hither qualities of closeness craving can be extremely attractive and seductive. However, once a committed relationship has been established, the wave can begin to perceive threats of rejection, withdrawal, or punishment—whether real or imagined. The wave's overly sensitized anticipation of rejection may result in rejecting his or her partner, and the inability to rekindle love.

Consuela, a wave, saw her romance with Jose as a dream come true. He (also a wave) was dashing, engaging, and fun loving. Their sex was, in her words, "amazing!" She was head-over-heels in love.

After the couple married, Consuela began to notice Jose making what she considered to be small shifts away from their close physical contact. For example, one evening at their favorite restaurant, they were talking about going to visit her parents the following weekend, when Jose suddenly broke all eye contact.

Consuela noticed immediately, but didn't say anything because she was afraid he might use it as an excuse not to visit her family. She knew he didn't enjoy being with them as often as she did.

Later that night as they were getting into bed, however, she couldn't keep her concerns to herself. "Why did you pull away at dinner?" she demanded.

Jose looked startled. "What are you talking about?"

"When we were discussing the visit to my parents. You wouldn't look me in the eye."

"Huh? I was looking at you. I *always* look at you." When Consuela insisted he wasn't meeting her eyes, Jose got defensive. "Well, I was taking the bones out of my fish," he said. "You want me to choke to death?"

Consuela turned out the light, got into bed, and turned her back to Jose. "What happened?" she silently despaired. "What did I do to cause this change?"

Other confrontations followed. Each time, Jose vehemently denied any negative feelings toward her. He insisted he loved her more than before they married.

But Consuela didn't believe him. She began to see in his eyes rejection and withdrawal, even though he protested to the contrary. She withdrew from him, sometimes angrily, in an effort to punish him for his supposed punishments of her. When he tried to look into her eyes, she looked away. Instead, she took to scanning the environment for eyes seeking hers. She felt good about herself when she was acknowledged by men who appeared smitten or at least interested in her. Eventually, this led to an affair with Armand, a dashing older man, who persuaded her to move in with him. She did so believing she had rediscovered the excitement of newfound love she once had with Jose.

It didn't take long, however, for this relationship to deteriorate. Just as had happened in her marriage, Consuela now saw disdain in Armand's previously adoring eyes. In her attempt to reconcile with Jose, she agreed to enter couple therapy. With the help of a therapist, they were able to understand their destructive wave inclinations and rekindle their love.

# NINTH GUIDING PRINCIPLE

The ninth principle in this book is that *partners can rekindle their love at any time through eye contact*. You do this by calling on your and your partner's primitives and ambassadors to intentionally engage in the same ways as when you were first enamored. This may sound deceptively simple, yet the results can be profound. What you are doing is tantamount to short-circuiting your brain's predisposition to war. If you haven't already attempted to rewire in this way, I suggest you reserve judgment until you have given it a fair try.

In the meantime, here are some supporting principles to guide you:

1. Don't be shy. Some people are naturally bashful when it comes to someone—even a loved one—looking freely into their eyes. This is especially true of islands, but some anchors and waves also are unaccustomed to extensive eye contact. I encourage you to push your limits with this. At the same time, allow yourselves to ease into it if one or

both of you feels shy. If the discomfort persists, investigate what is keeping you from feeling safe and secure with each other.

2. Vary your approach. I stress eye contact because of its great potential to rekindle love. But the other near senses are powerful, as well. You may want to turn the I See You exercise into I Touch You, or even try it with the senses of smell and taste.

3. Don't wait. If you wait to try rekindling love through eye contact until a fight has erupted with your partner, it may be too late, at least for that instance. You want to practice ahead of time, when tensions are low. The point is to find ways to rewire so your ambassadors are pre-disposed to come online before your primitives. Then, when tensions do rise, that more loving response will be second nature to you

CHAPTER 10

# Live a Happier, Healthier Life: How Your Partnership Can Heal You

Imagine that the plumbing in your house has a slow leak, and you haven't checked your monthly water bill in, say, thirty years. Now you look at it, and you're stunned! It's not just that you let the leak continue for so long, but the amount of water you wasted over time is enormous.

Now suppose it were possible to similarly measure energy usage in your body. Imagine that your stress system hasn't been checked since infancy to see how much energy you have expended adapting to life's various stresses. Additionally, take into account the fact that some of this energy is nonrenewable. That is, it has seeped away over time due to stress, and like the water from that leaky pipe, can't be retrieved.

The "bill" you receive for your total stress expenditures is what Bruce McEwen (2000) and other scientists call *allostatic load*, otherwise known as the price we pay for the adaptations required of us throughout life. Allostatic load involves four major physiological systems: cardiovascular, autoimmune, inflammatory, and metabolic. Over time, if we accumulate a heavy allostatic load, we can develop illness in any or all of these four systems, including heart disease, diabetes, arthritis, and fibromyalgia.

Our relationships with others, and especially our primary committed relationship, strongly influence our allostatic load, by either reducing or increasing it. Yes, it can work both ways, and which way it works for you is largely up to you. Some individuals—islands for example, but also many waves—choose to forego relationships, at least primary ones, in favor of solitude because they find committed relationships too stressful. They may avoid stress, but they avoid closeness, as well. Others readily pursue relationships, only to find themselves feeling abused, neglected, or otherwise dispirited by the realities of their marriage or union. The stress they encounter in their relationship puts them at risk for illness. Still others find themselves in relationships that help them thrive, energize, and destress.

This chapter focuses on the health hazards as well as the health benefits that come with a primary relationship. As you read it, consider what you might do to ensure that your relationship mitigates stress and always contributes to your greater health and happiness.

# THE HAZARDS OF HIDDEN STRESS

If you ask a couple to identify the main sources of stress in their lives, chances are they won't point to their relationship. In many cases, that answer is exactly as it should be. However, for some couples, this represents a blind spot. Although they may be alert to stress in other areas of their lives, such as stress caused by a boss at work or financial problems, they are in denial when it comes to stress in their relationship.

Ralph and Lorraine have been together for more than thirty years. Midway in their marriage, both made explicit and implicit suggestions that the very existence of the relationship was in continuous question. For example, when they fought, Ralph would say, "If you don't quit yelling, you won't have anyone to yell at anymore!" Later, he'd say, "I don't know, maybe I'm just not cut out for this marriage thing."

When she was angry, Lorraine would say, "If you pull that pathetic crap one more time, I swear, I'm out of here!"

During this time, two of their three children began to manifest symptoms of depression and anxiety. Lorraine started to become physically symptomatic, with a range of inexplicable illnesses. Her immune system was compromised, and she too became depressed. Ralph, who had a family history of heart disease, started to frequent the emergency room with complaints of heart palpitations.

Fortunately, Ralph and Lorraine were able in therapy to get to the bottom of what was making them sick. Life was hard enough, but it was even more difficult because each lived under constant threat—both to the relationship and their sense of self. This might seem obvious, but to Ralph and Lorraine it wasn't. They were entrenched in their habits and didn't realize the effects their behavior was having on everyone in the family. They didn't recognize how they were increasing each other's allostatic load. In addition to outright threats, they treated one another with contempt and disgust.

Ralph and Lorraine agreed to stop their threatening behaviors, and when they did, something miraculous happened. Lorraine's health improved almost immediately, as did her depression. Ralph stopped experiencing heart palpitations. The children appeared happier and better adjusted at home, at school, and in their social life. Lorraine and Ralph still argued and complained about one another, but they no longer threatened the relationship or each other.

## BE ANNOYING BUT NEVER THREATENING

I often tell couples that within their couple bubble they can do or say things that are annoying, but they can never be threatening in the eyes of their partner. You can be annoying with a smile on your face, and laugh about it later. But threats undercut your very security. Moreover, it doesn't really matter what *you* consider threatening; if your behavior is perceived as threatening by your partner, then you have a problem. That said, here are some behaviors that typically are considered threatening:

♥ Raging

♥ Hitting or other forms of violence

♥ Threats against the relationship

♥ Threats against the person

♥ Threats against others important to your partner

♥ Holding on for too long and not letting go

♥ Refusing to repair or make right a wrong

♥ Withdrawing for periods longer than an hour or two

- ♥ Being consistently unapologetic

- ♥ Behaving habitually in an unfair or unjust manner

- ♥ Putting self-serving interests ahead of the relationship too much of the time

- ♥ Expressing contempt (devaluation; e.g., "you're a moron")

- ♥ Expressing disgust (loathing or repulsion; e.g., "you make me sick")

Lynn Katz and John Gottman (1993) studied the deleterious effects of partners' expressions of contempt and found that not only does this behavior put the relationship at risk, but it has a disruptive influence on their children's behavior. Gottman (2004) ranks contempt, which he defines as including disgust, disrespect, condescension, and sarcasm, as the number one predictor of divorce.

If any of the behaviors listed apply to your relationship, then you or your partner are a threat to live with, and ultimately destructive to your collective wish to remain safe and secure. Remember, partners are wired together: where one goes, so goes the other. If you are threatening or if your partner feels threatened, or vice versa, it can't be good for you, either. You owe it to your relationship to immediately eliminate all threatening behavior. If this means seeking the help of a therapist, as in the case of Ralph and Lorraine, I can't think of a better investment you could make in your relationship.

## EXERCISE: SEEING THE BLIND SPOTS

Do you think you might have a blind spot when it comes to the level of stress at home? If you answer yes to the following, stress may be hurting your relationship.

1. Do you or others in your family have frequent and unexplained physical ailments, such as digestive problems, insomnia, chronic pain, chronic fatigue, or allergies? Any autoimmune or inflammatory problems?

2. Are you or others in your family suffering from depression or anxiety, or emotional overload?

3. Do you or your partner say or do things that could be perceived as threatening?

4. Do you and your partner fight frequently?

I realize these may be tough questions to ask. But if you don't ask, you risk losing not only your relationship but your health and well-being.

# HEALING WITHIN THE COUPLE BUBBLE

It's not enough to minimize stress at home: your relationship can and should serve as your strongest force for health and well-being. Consider how another couple handled this issue.

Susi and Tamara came from families that did not provide much physical contact or nurturing. Neither remembers being hugged, held, rocked, or kissed as a child. As an adult couple, Susi and Tamara were good friends and thought well of one another and the relationship. They had the occasional argument, but neither ever threatened the other. Essentially, they lived parallel lives and rarely made physical contact. They slept in different rooms and weren't affectionate or huggy.

Both Susi and Tamara complained of almost continuous anxiety, but neither seemed good at calming or soothing the other. It never occurred to them that their physical distance and lack of physical comforting came with a price tag. Tamara had fibromyalgia and Epstein-Barr syndrome, which worsened as she aged. Susi had numerous health problems, including irritable bowel syndrome, diabetes, obesity, and joint pain.

When this couple eventually discovered in therapy that their lack of contact contributed to their health woes, change did not come easily. Because they were unheld babies, each had strong aversion reactions to close physical contact. Although they never became as affectionate as many other couples, they took steps to develop a couple bubble for the first time. They started to sleep in the same room and made time to cuddle at night. Surprisingly quickly, these changes resulted in reduced physical complaints from both Susi and Tamara.

## WE ALL NEED TO BE TOUCHED

We have known, scientifically speaking, since the 1950s, that every child needs touch, holding, and rocking. Harry Harlow (1958) and others, such as James Prescott (1975), famously studied rhesus baby monkeys and found a stronger drive for physical comfort than for food. Others, such as John Bowlby (1969), Margaret Mahler and her colleagues (Mahler, Pine, and Bergman 2000), and David Stern (1998) found identical needs in human infants and children. And these needs continue into adulthood. We all need to be touched, hugged, held, and (at times) rocked by another. Even under minor stress, our primitives will not fully settle if touch is unavailable to us.

Do you remember the study I mentioned in chapter 2 about the London cabbies whose hippocampus grew larger on the job? Well, a recent study by Brigitte Apfel and her team (2011) found that Gulf War veterans suffering from chronic stress had a smaller hippocampus than did veterans who had recovered from stress. One interpretation of this finding is that our hippocampus actually shrinks when we are under stress for an extended time. Not only does the hippocampus regulate our stress response, but chronic stress appears to inhibit its ability to control the release of stress hormones. While you're unlikely to ever determine the size of your hippocampus, all this goes to say it's valuable to know something we may take for granted—such as the amount of time spent touching or hugging—can have measurable neurobiological consequences. Moreover, giving each other the touch you need may well have the capacity to reverse damages.

---

## EXERCISE: BE MEDICINE FOR EACH OTHER

How much time do you and your partner spend in close physical contact? I don't mean just making love; that's part of it, of course, but there's much more: hugging, holding each other, cuddling, holding hands, kissing, giving a massage, and so on. Contact in these ways is not only enjoyable, it serves as actual medicine for both of you—to help your body heal, and as a preventive means to maintain your health.

If you haven't already, I suggest you add this to your daily routine over the next week.

1. Find a time when you can be alone together for a minimum of ten minutes every day. It can be before you go to sleep, or any other time that's convenient.

2. Spend this time in close physical contact. No sex! You can cuddle, caress, or even cradle one another as you would a baby. If you are someone who feels uneasy with physical contact, do this anyway and talk about it with your partner. Chances are high that you have always been touch aversive. But that doesn't mean you need to stay this way. Right? We're talking about your health here.

3. Notice the effect this time has on your level of stress and on your physical health. Although you may want to continue beyond one week to realize the full effect, I'd be surprised if you don't notice any benefits even within these first few days.

---

# TENTH GUIDING PRINCIPLE

The tenth principle is that *partners can minimize each other's stress and optimize each other's health.* I find this fitting for the closing of this book because it in effect ties together what we have already discussed. Bottom line, by adhering to the principles presented in the previous chapters—for example, a couple bubble based in true mutuality, well-trained ambassadors that keep your primitives in check, an up-to-date owner's manual for your relationship—you avoid causing stress to yourself and your partner. In so doing, you actively foster physical and emotional health and well-being for both of you.

Here are some supporting principles to guide you:

1. Manage each other's stress. In recent decades, techniques for stress reduction have become increasingly popular. You may already be familiar with these—time management, eating regular meals, getting enough sleep, exercising, relaxation, to name a few. However, what's missing in most approaches to stress management is the key role partners can play. I'm suggesting that, as experts on one another who

understand something about how your brains function, you can add the dimension of stress reduction to your owner's manual. Knowing the three or four things that make your partner feel bad gives you an advantage when it comes to detecting stress and even anticipating it.

You and your partner can support one another in reducing stress by making sure you engage in healthy activities and achieve balance in your lifestyle. If you notice your partner isn't getting enough sleep, for example, step in and help find a solution. You might volunteer to take on extra household chores until he or she has caught up on needed rest. If your partner is slacking in his or her exercise routine, this might be the time to go to the gym together. Or if your partner had a hard day at work, maybe tonight is the right evening to rent that comedy you've talked about watching.

2. Be aware of the unique experience of stress. As you help manage your partner's stress, keep in mind that everyone experiences stress in a different way. For example, a tax audit that causes you to lose sleep could be seen by your partner as a minor blip on the radar. In this case, you each bring a different history and set of feelings about financial matters. So be careful not to impose your own evaluation of stress on your partner. Remember, you are an expert on him or her. So when you help your partner reduce stress, you do so on his or her terms. And, of course, your partner will reciprocate in kind.

3. As you age.... Not all illness is caused by stress, but stress can aggravate any illness and make it worse. As you and your partner age, you inevitably will encounter the natural challenges all our bodies face as the years advance. Know, however, that by loving one another fully, learning how to defuse conflict and make choices that are pro-relationship rather than pro-self, and wiring yourselves for love, you stand the best chance of enjoying a happy, healthy, and ultimately satisfying union.

# Postscript

When all is said and done, most of us are doing the best we can, and most of us don't go into relationships with the intention of messing things up. We try our best to love and be loved in return. Yet despite our best intentions, when we do mess things up, it most likely is because we disregarded, dismissed, or didn't know about at least one of the principles described in this book.

This should give hope to the reader because, the truth is, you can still be wired for love, if not in this relationship, then in the next one. It is never too late. And there is no one reading this book who can't ultimately do it right.

Thankfully, relationships are not like baseball, in which it's three strikes and you're out. Couples have more options, and more resources at their fingertips. The universe keeps pitching us new opportunities to redo, repair, and reinvent ourselves in relationship to another person, perhaps even the same person. We just need to envision a more principled reason to be together, a more life-enhancing purpose to devote ourselves to another person. This purpose must be based on true mutuality; on giving ourselves fully to our chosen other; and on the willingness to accept one another as we are, with all our irritating qualities.

# References

Ainsworth, M. D. S., S. M. Bell, and D. J. Stayton. 1971. Individual differences in strange situation behavior of one year olds. In *The origins of human social relations*, edited by H. R. Schaffer, 17–57. New York: Academic Press.

Apfel, B. A., J. Ross, J. Hlavin, D. J. Meyerhoff, T. J. Metzler, C. R. Marmar, M. W. Weiner, N. Schuff, and T. C. Neylan. 2011. Hippocampal volume differences in Gulf War veterans with current versus lifetime posttraumatic stress disorder symptoms. *Biological Psychiatry* 69(6):541–548.

Bowlby, J. 1969. *Attachment and Loss*. New York: Basic Books.

Dittami, J., M. Keckeis, I. Machatschke, S. Katina, J. Zeitlhofer, and G. Kloesch. 2007. Sex differences in the reactions to sleeping in pairs versus sleeping alone in humans. *Sleep and Biological Rhythms* 5(4):271–276.

Fisher, H. E., A. Aron, and L. L. Brown. 2005. Romantic love: An fMRI study of a neural mechanism for mate choice. *The Journal of Comparative Neurology* 493(1):58–62.

Gottman, J., and N. Silver. 2004. *The Seven Principles for Making Marriage Work*. London: Orion.

Hanson, R., and R. Mendius. 2009. *Buddha's Brain: The Practical Neuroscience of Happiness, Love, and Wisdom*. Oakland, CA: New Harbinger.

Harlow, H. 1958. The nature of love. *American Psychologist* 13:673–685.

Katz, L. F., and Gottman, J. M. 1993. Patterns of marital conflict predict children's internalizing and externalizing behaviors. *Developmental Psychology,* 29(6):940–950.

Kiecolt-Glaser J. K., T. J. Loving, J. R. Stowell, W. B. Malarkey, S. Lemeshow, S. L. Dickinson, and R. Glaser. 2005. Hostile marital interactions, proinflammatory cytokine production, and wound healing. *The Archives of General Psychiatry* 62(12):1377–1384.

Larson, J. H., D. Crane, and C. W. Smith. 1991. Morning and night couples: The effect of wake and sleep patterns on marital adjustment. *Journal of Marital & Family Therapy* 17(1):53–65.

Lucas, R. E., and A. E. Clark. 2006. Do people really adapt to marriage? *Journal of Happiness Studies* 7:405–426. doi: 10.1007/s10902-006-9001-x

MacLean, P. D. 1996. Women: A more balanced brain? *Zygon* 31(3):421–439. doi: doi:10.1111/j.1467-9744.1996.tb00035.x

Maguire, E. A., D. G. Gadian, I. S. Johnsrude, C. D. Good, J. Ashburner, R. S. Frackowiak, and C. D. Frith. 2000. Navigation-related structural change in the hippocampi of taxi drivers. *Proceedings of the National Academy of Sciences* 97(8):4398–403. doi:10.1073/pnas.070039597.

Mahler, M. S., F. Pine, and A. Bergman. 2000. *The Psychological Birth of the Human Infant Symbiosis and Individuation.* New York: Basic Books.

McEwen, B. S. 2000. "Allostasis and allostatic load: implications for neuropsychopharmacology" *Neuropsychopharmacology* 22(2):108–24. doi:10 .1016/S0893-133X(99)00129-3

Pakkenberg, B., and H. Gundersen. 1997. Neocortical neuron number in humans: Effect of sex and age. *The Journal of Comparative Neurology* 384(2):312–320.

Porges S. W. 1995. Orienting in a defensive world: Mammalian modifications of our evolutionary heritage. A Polyvagal Theory. *Psychophysiology* 32: 301–318.

Prescott, J. W. 1975. Body pleasure and the origins of violence. *Bulletin of Atomic Scientists* (Nov.):10–20.

Sapolsky, R. M. 2004. *Why Zebras Don't Get Ulcers* (3rd ed.). New York: Holt.

Smith, T. 2006. *American Sexual Behavior: Trends, Socio-demographic Differences, and Risk Behavior.* Chicago, IL: University of Chicago National Opinion Research Center.

Stern, D. N. 1998. *The Interpersonal World of the Infant: A View from Psychoanalysis and Developmental Psychology.* London, UK: Karnac Books.

Stern, D. N. 2004. *The Present Moment in Psychotherapy and Everyday Life.* New York: Norton.

Stutzer, A., and B. S. Frey. 2003. Does marriage make people happy, or do happy people get married? *The Journal of Socio Economics* 35(2). 326–347.

Troxel, Wendy M. 2010. It's more than sex: Exploring the dyadic nature of sleep and implications for health. *Psychosomatic Medicine* 72(6):578–586. doi:10.1097/PSY.0b013e3181de7ff8

Waite, L., and M. Gallagher. 2000. *The Case for Marriage: Why Married People Are Happier, Healthier, and Better Off Financially.* New York: Doubleday.

Weaver, J. 2007. Many cheat for a thrill, more stay true for love. Accessed September 5, 2011. http://www.msnbc.msn.com/id/17951664/ns/health-sexual_health/

Winnicott, D. W. 1957. *Mother and Child: A Primer of First Relationships.* New York: Basic Books.

**Stan Tatkin, PsyD,** is assistant clinical professor in the family medicine department at the University of California, Los Angeles and is on the adjunct faculty of the masters psychology program at Antioch University in Santa Barbara, the masters psychology program at the California Lutheran University of Thousand Oaks, and the doctoral pre- and perinatal psychology program at Santa Barbara Graduate Institute. He teaches and supervises family medicine residents at Kaiser Permanente in Woodland Hills and is the creator of the psychobiological approach to couple therapy, or PACT. He is coauthor of *Love and War in Intimate Relationships.* He lives with his wife and daughter in Calabasas, CA.

Foreword writer **Harville Hendrix, PhD,** is a clinical pastoral counselor and cocreator of imago relationship therapy. He has more than thirty-five years of experience as an educator, public lecturer, and couples' therapist. He is author of numerous books, including *Getting the Love You Want.*